HEALTHY EATING ON A LOW BUDGET

HEALTHY EATING ON A LOW BUDGET

Maggie Black

BLANDFORD PRESS
POOLE·NEW YORK·SYDNEY

First published in the UK 1986 by Blandford Press
Link House, West Street, Poole, Dorset BH15 1LL

British Library Cataloguing in Publication Data

Black, Maggie
  Healthy eating on a low budget.
  1. Cookery (Natural foods)   2. Low budget cookery
  I. Title
  641.5′637   TX741

ISBN 0 7137 1570 7

Typeset by Poole Typesetting (Wessex) Ltd

Printed in Great Britain by Biddles Ltd., Guildford

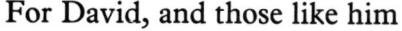

For David, and those like him

CONTENTS

ACKNOWLEDGMENTS

This book has been possible through the research of many scientists, nutritionists and dietitians over the years. In writing about their findings, I have been helped immensely by the generous guidance of Pat Howard S.R.D. who, despite her senior full-time work, has supplied me with vital research material and statistics, and has brought her expert knowledge to bear when reading and commenting on the text of this book. Her suggestions – and warnings – have been invaluable. On some aspects of the currently complex problem of the role of dietary fats, I also owe much thanks to Dr Laurence Knights B.M., B.Sc. for similar guidance. As a result, any errors which remain lie at my own door.

Many other people and more books have also contributed to my knowledge, and my writing. Regretfully, I cannot mention them all; but I would like to single out Mary Ann Logan and Sue Black for supplying American and Australian references, Pat Knights for testing and tasting many of the recipes, and my unflaggingly patient typists, Judy Pointer, Sarah Robson and Adeline Hain. As for authors of nutrition and low-cost cookery books, I want to acknowledge the influence, especially, of my good friend Theodora Fitzgibbon whose cooking for health and economy is always wise, of Rose Elliot in England and Vic Sussman in the USA as imaginative vegetarians, and of Christine Lewis for many ideas in her book *The Food Choice Jungle*. To my publisher and editor, I want also to say thank you, not only for patiently unravelling my messy, oft-amended scripts, but for stimulating me to write a book which has changed my own way of eating and thereby improved my health remarkably. I am also indebted to Her Majesty's Stationery Office for permission to publish material from *Recommended Daily Amounts of Food Energy and Nutrients for Groups of People in the United Kingdom, 1979, The Composition of Foods by A.A. Paul and D.A.T. Southgate, 1978* and *Manual of Nutrition*, Ministry of Agriculture, Fisheries and Food, 1976.

Maggie Black 1986

PART 1
NUTRITION AND
DIET

Throughout Part 1, an asterisk (*) against the name of a dish indicates
that the recipe can be found in Part 2.

1. YOU ARE WHAT YOU EAT

'You are what you eat' is pretty well true where your everyday health is concerned. You can prove it for yourself quite easily. All of us know people who fall victim to stomach disorders as soon as they go to a strange, warmer climate, although the local inhabitants never suffer from it. Oily or acid foods, and unfamiliar spices or microbes in the food and water are the gremlins in this case.

More sneakily, your usual foods may leave you vulnerable to various ills, if they do not provide you with all the nutrients you need, in the right proportions or 'mix'.

Nutrients are the various types of food material which, working together, keep you alive. There are six of them.
1) *Proteins* provide materials for building and repairing the body tissues.
2) *Carbohydrates* provide much of the energy needed for all the body's activities and functions.
3) *Fats and Oils* also supply energy, and keep the body warm; besides this, they contain certain essential vitamins.
4) *Vitamins* help to provide protection from disease and keep the body's processes functioning well.
5) *Minerals*; some provide building materials and others regulate some of the body's processes.
6) *Water* forms a main part of all the body's cells, and most of its secretions; it also transports materials within the body, and helps to regulate its temperature.

Fibre also forms an important part of many foodstuffs because it regulates bowel movement, and is a 'carrier' of nutrients, although it is not a nutrient itself.

If your body goes short of any type of nutrient, your health soon suffers. You feel less energetic and alert than you should, and are more liable to get ailments such as colds and 'flu. You are also likely to enjoy life less. It may become too much trouble to cook a good meal or to dress up for a party; the kids' or the neighbours' noise gets on your nerves. You may not feel ill enough to go to bed, but just off colour; nonetheless, you slow up and act less effectively than if you felt in top form. You tend to put off doing things, and to make mistakes.

No one can afford this state of affairs, especially if living on a low budget. You need your wits about you – if you are looking for a job or trying to hold one down, for instance, or want to make the most of your retirement.

It can spoil your chances. Yet the cause may just be that your food lacks the right nutrients to give you the punch and drive to get the most out of life. Everyone needs both the protection against ill-health and the positive extra well-being that fully nourishing good food gives.

Almost all foods contain a mixture of nutrients. Your body gets them as you digest your meals because the digestive juices in your mouth, stomach and intestines break down the various foods into simple nutrient forms which your body can absorb. But no single food contains all the nutrients you need to keep your body in good repair and functioning well. So proper nourishment consists of eating a variety of foods which, between them, contain the right quantities of all the nutrients you need. This assortment of foods makes up what we call a healthy diet.

In the next six chapters we will look at what the different kinds of nutrients do for us, and at the other vital constituent of our food – fibre.

2. PROTEINS

Protein does the obviously vital job, which no other nutrient can do, of building the body's tissues (flesh, blood, bones, hair, and so on) and of repairing them when needed. You could not live without it.

This means, literally, that you have to eat to live, because human beings, like animals, cannot get the various kinds of protein they need in any other way.

Fish, meat, cheese, eggs and milk are foods packed with protein which our bodies can use easily. Even without knowing this, many people think that it is essential to eat fish, poultry or, in particular, meat every day if they are to be nourished properly. These are the most expensive food items one can choose. Yet, although they must scrimp and save, many people try to put on the table a main meal of butcher's meat or poultry almost every day, with fish occasionally as a change.

They look on pasta, rice, beans and most vegetables just as 'fillers' without much food value.

This seems an odd way of thinking, because nearly every sizeable city in the English-speaking world now has at least one oriental restaurant or 'take-away', and even people who often patronise them do not seem to suffer without their steak and French fries. Many members of the Asian communities in such towns are vegetarians, yet they live active lives on rice-based, meatless meals. A good many rooted Westerners themselves are also turning to being wholly or partly vegetarian, apparently without any ill effects. What do all these people do to get enough of the various kinds of protein?

PROTEINS IN PLANTS

The answer is that there are also many different proteins in plant foods, such as beans and nuts, although most of them cannot be used by human beings as they stand. Luckily, every protein, whether in animal or plant food, consists largely of simpler substances called amino-acids, linked together like different-coloured beads on a chain, in a special pattern or order; for instance, blue, green, purple, red. Each protein has its own, unique amino-acid 'bead' pattern; no two are alike.

As you digest your food, the various proteins are broken down into a general collection or 'bank' of amino-acids from which your body can pick up and link together the particular amino-acids for the proteins it wants – provided certain essential ones are there in the 'bank' to start with.

Adults have eight of these essential amino-acids. All the others in the protein patterns useful to human beings can be swapped around – rather like substituting mauve 'beads' for purple if the 'bank' has no purple ones. But these ones must be in a protein's amino-acid 'bead' pattern themselves, to make it of any use to us. No wonder we call them essential amino-acids!

Meat, fish, cheese, eggs and milk contain all the essential amino-acids. So do one or two plant foods such as soya beans and peanuts. Some other plant foods contain proteins which have quite a good supply of most essential amino-acids, and only need one or two more to turn them into usable protein foods. Wholemeal (whole wheat) bread, for instance, contains excellent, although incomplete, protein. Soaked and cooked dried beans contain it too, and so do potatoes.

Now, here is the interesting part. Beans and other pulses have the amino-acids missing in the whole-grain flour and other cereal foods; so if you eat beans and whole-grain bread together at the same meal, they give you almost the same 'mix' of amino-acids as when you eat meat. Canned baked beans on toast makes a first-class protein meal – and is a whole lot cheaper than steak.

You can make excellent pocket-saving use of the proteins in grain plants in another way, unless you are a strict vegetarian. Even a very small quantity of cheese, fish, eggs, yoghurt or milk (including semi-skimmed and skimmed milk) will make up for the missing amino-acids in the plant proteins.

Eggs not only have all the essential amino-acids, but more than we need of some of them; they 'marry' especially well with potatoes to make first-class cheap protein dishes. Compare the cost of Eggs in Potato Nests* with that of grilled pork chops, for instance.

The foods which complement each other must be eaten in the same meal (although not always in the same course) because your body does not 'store' its amino-acids.

On the following page you will find a list of some cheap and easy dishes which mix these foods to give you a good supply of protein.

CHEAP PROTEIN DISHES WITHOUT MEAT
Thick lentil or pea soup with wholemeal (whole wheat) toast or oatcakes★
Minestrone (made with whole wheat pasta and peas)
Sautéed potatoes with scrambled eggs
Baked Stuffed Potatoes★
Eggs in Potato Nests★
Mixed Vegetables in Potato Rings★
Kedgeree (made with brown rice and peas)
Risotto (made with brown rice and peas)
Curried beans or lentils with brown rice
Wholemeal (whole wheat) pasta with Tomato Sauce★ and grated cheese
Boston baked beans followed by muesli with yoghurt
Wholemeal (whole wheat) Bean Croquettes★
Cheese and potato pie
Sweetcorn or Lentil Patties★

N.B. You will find recipes for most of these dishes in any good standard cookery book, and the starred ones in Part 2.

If you want to, you can use any of the suggestions above for a main dish instead of meat, either regularly or just when the budget really pinches. You will be just as well nourished.

USING PLANT PROTEINS
Some people are put off cooking bean or grain dishes because they think that they are more trouble to prepare than meat and take longer to cook. But this is not true on the whole. Granted, some dried beans may need soaking, and simmering for hours, but this involves no more thinking ahead than shopping, and they need no attention while cooking. Except for soya beans, they will keep for 2–3 days in a cool place if you have not got a refrigerator, and they reheat perfectly, so you can cook enough for 2 or 3 meals at once. If you are really 'stuck' for time or cooking facilities, canned beans, although more expensive than dried ones to buy, are still good value. For some good ways to use them which won't break the bank, see page 00.

As for pasta and rice, they cook just as quickly as grilling a chop or ham slice and they keep and reheat perfectly too. What's more, you can vary the flavourings easily; it is really not difficult to grate a little cheese over macaroni, or to mix in a small can of tomatoes or peas when reheating it – and the saucepan will be a lot less trouble to wash up than a greasy grill or frying pan, or the pot in which you have made a meat stew.

14

Remember, too, that pasta and grains save you shopping time and fares because they can be kept 'on the shelf' as an ever-ready backstop. With a few cans or packets to supplement them, say, canned tomatoes, freeze-dried peas and dried skimmed milk, you have got all the ingredients for a meal right at hand. This can be a boon, for instance to elderly people in bad weather, or to a harassed mother with a sick child.

Another thing puts some people off: the bulk of the starchy vegetable-protein foods. You have to eat a lot more risotto than roast chicken to get the same amount of usable protein; perhaps more than you can manage at one sitting. Many people, these days, especially if on a tight budget, just have one 'real' meal a day, and snack meals such as sandwiches or perhaps just coffee and biscuits at other times. If the main meal consists of a starchy vegetable dish, surely they run the risk of being undernourished.

Certainly this would be a deficient diet on several grounds if the snack meals or light snacks, and any 'afters' at the main meal have little food value. But luckily it is quite difficult not to get enough protein if you use a little commonsense.

For instance, if you have a small appetite as many elderly people have, you can spread your day's protein intake over two light or snack meals instead of one large one, provided both contain a protein mixture; say a hard-boiled (hard-cooked) egg salad at lunch-time and baked beans on toast for supper. Alternatively, a wholemeal (whole wheat) bread and cheese sandwich with 275 ml/$\frac{1}{2}$ pt ($1\frac{1}{4}$ cups) milk could provide a good part of the needed protein at midday, while a small can of sardines, drained and mashed on toast for supper could provide the rest. The milk could be used for both a small glassful and for milky coffee or tea at the second meal.

You can use this way of getting your protein just as easily if you are young and, say, an office worker. For instance, if you want to shop in your lunch-hour instead of sitting over a meal, you could have a fruit yoghurt (better still, plain yoghurt and an apple) at a fast-food counter and buy a packet of peanuts as 'afters'. Then if you are going to a show after work, get a chicken sandwich or 'burger in a bun on the way.

You can find out a good deal more about this 'small meal' pattern and how snack meals differ from low-value 'nibbles' in Chapter 9 in the section on menu-making.

Whether you try this way of eating or not, it is useful to remember that you need not get all your protein from savoury dishes. For a family, a good many sweet desserts such as Rice Pudding (made with brown rice), Brown Betty* or a cheesecake have good protein value. For one person, muesli with milk supplies protein; so do some baked goods such as Peanut Butter Cookies*.

15

HOW MUCH PROTEIN?

How much protein should you eat in a day? This can be a tricky question. The amount of protein each person needs varies. Your particular protein requirement depends on, for instance, your sex, how old you are, the way in which your body functions chemically, and the kinds of protein and other foods which you eat at the same meal.

The total amount of nourishment in any food is measured in the units of energy popularly called calories, strictly kilocalories (Kcal) or kilojoules (Kj). Most diet books contain tables which give the average number of calories in various foods. However, some of these tables vary a great deal in the number of calories they suggest. Moreover, they are not really helpful if we want to measure protein alone, because no food which we normally eat consists only of protein. It is always mixed with 'carrier' material and with other nutrients such as the carbohydrates in pulses, the fat in cheese or the mineral element calcium in milk. The actual quantity of usable protein (or any other nutrient) in 25 g/1 oz of the food may be very small. (In fact, for convenience, all nutrients are normally measured just in grams or the smaller milligrams [mg], or even tinier micrograms [mcg], without their equivalents in ounces which as units are much larger than grams [strictly, 1 oz is equivalent to 28.35 grams]. One gram of usable protein provies 4.1 calories.)

Modern medical research seems to show that, on a Western diet, we all need less protein than we used to think, although some special groups of people need to take a larger percentage of their calories in the form of protein than the rest of us. Pregnant and nursing mothers, tiny babies, children and teenagers who are still growing fast all need plenty of protein. So does anyone who takes hard physical exercise. Anyone who has had an operation or injury, or a wasting disease, also needs extra good supplies of protein.

Table 1 in Appendix II shows the average daily calorie and protein needs of various groups of people. This comes from a British Government report on recommended food energy and nutrient quantitites which is described in Chapter 9. From this table, you can see about how much pure protein the average person *should* eat every day as a rule, at different ages. However, your need as an individual may differ from the average a good deal; and besides that, the figures obviously cannot tell you whether you *are* in fact eating about the right amount, neither too little nor wastefully too much. For that, you have to work out the amount of usable protein in every food you eat on an ordinary day.

This is very difficult because although some cartons and cans tell you the nutrient values of the foods inside them, the only way to find out these values in most everyday foods is to consult a book of special tables; and even then, like the suggested desirable calorie and protein intakes, the figures given only represent average values. Actual values may vary a lot, depending on the season, the quality of the product, and so on. Nor is that all. The quantity of any nutrient which you as an individual actually absorb can also vary, depending on a great many factors such as the various types of food you eat at a particular meal.

If, for medical reasons, you need an accurate assessment or a special high or low protein diet, your doctor will prescribe one. Otherwise, let commonsense guide you. Ordinary modest Western-style meals provide quite sensible protein intakes for most people.

SPECIAL NEEDS

If you belong to one of the special groups mentioned on p.16 or have a child to care for, make doubly sure of your own or your child's protein intake. If you have been ill or injured, you probably have access to medical advice; and in a Western society you should be able to get advice concerning a schoolgoing child's or teenager's diet from a local authority clinic or community or school health worker. But if you are a mother breast-feeding a young baby, you may not feel you need, or can afford, a special high-protein diet for yourself, especially if you feel well. Do not be lulled into carelessness by that, or by the fact that what you are doing is normal and natural. You need extra protein even more than before your baby was born. To make sure that your infant develops strong bones and teeth, you should have plenty of milk, to make sure you get the protein you need in a compact 'package' with bone-building calcium. Take it in the concentrated form of cheese if you prefer it to liquid milk; you can team it with bread or potatoes in several different ways, to make up for the higher cost. (If you have an elderly person to care for, make sure that he or she gets enough cheese or milk too. Old people tend to have small appetites and brittle bones. See page 108-10.)

VARIETY IS IMPORTANT

To get all the benefit of the protein you eat, you need to eat some carbohydrate with it, either in the same foodstuff 'package' or at the same time. Do not fall into the 'slimmer's' trap of grabbing a cooked chicken leg from the fridge for your packed office lunch and nothing else, to make sure of your protein while avoiding 'fattening' bread or biscuits. Carbo-hydrate's main job is to supply energy. Without it, your body may not digest and absorb the chicken leg's protein properly.

This is just one of the good reasons for making starchy plant protein mixtures part of your protein intake. Your protein will not only cost less money, you will get the full value of every gram of it because the carbohydrate is 'built in' instead of being cooked separately and added. You save on work and fuel too.

Another good reason for choosing vegetable proteins sometimes is that they come 'packaged' with dietary fibre, which meat, fish, egg and dairy proteins do not. Provided you use wholemeal (whole-grain) products, you get a useful basic supply of essential fibre without any hassle. Chapter 6 explains why this supply is so important.

Some vegetable protein 'packages' make yet another contribution because they include valuable vitamins and minerals which may be absent from other foods in your meal. You can also make good use of such 'packages' to provide alternatives or supplements to some of the nutrients in animal foods. For instance, if someone in your family is a fussy eater, it may be a good idea to try to provide the important daily supply of certain vitamins and minerals (page 55) in two different dishes in the main meal; a whole-grain pudding is often a cheap and popular second choice.

The fact that plant proteins (and the protein in gelatine) lack some essential amino-acids does not destroy their value (p.13). (Any amino-acids which are in short supply or missing in one protein food can be supplied by any other which is rich in them.) Furthermore, by mixing them with animal proteins, we get the best out of *both*. The more varied the protein foods we eat, the more likely we are to get all the types and the quantities of amino-acids our bodies need at that time. So nutritionists consider that we make the fullest and best use of our protein foods by taking about half of them from animal products and half from plant sources, and by eating a mixture of both kinds at each meal.

Variety is important on another score. It is the 'spice' of life – certainly of healthy eating! Familiar routine dishes are 'safe', but varying them makes meals more interesting, provided the substitutes are flavoursome and colourful. It is well known that interesting, appealing food is digested more easily, which means that our bodies can make better use of it. The recipes in Part 2 will help you, I hope, to create an interesting variety of protein dishes.

GOOD VALUE PROTEIN FOODS TO USE
MILK
Dried whole, semi-skimmed and skimmed milk powders usually cost no more than fresh milk, and are useful 'shelf' products if you lack fridge

space. They have just as much protein as fresh milk when made up. Do not use them for babies.

EGGS
Medium or small (sizes 3 and 4) eggs are cheaper than large ones (sizes 1 and 2), and just as useful for most cooking. White eggs are cheaper than brown and just as nourishing. All eggs change in price with the seasons.

While eggs are an excellent protein food, and also supply calcium, phosphorus and Vitamins A and D, egg yolks are high in cholesterol (see page 34) so their use should be limited.

Make the most of your eggs by using them in savoury dishes and by making or buying cakes, cookies and pastry goods without eggs in them whenever you can. As a rule try not to use more than 3–4 egg yolks a week per person.

HARD CHEESE
Cheddar is the cheapest hard cheese for full flavour value. A little goes a long way when grated or in a sauce. Semi-hard and soft cheeses often have less protein, and so do cheese spreads. Spreads tend to be expensive for the food value they offer.

POTATOES
An excellent protein food with eggs, especially good value because you can cook them in so many different ways. Remember that much of their goodness lies in or just under the skin. Whenever possible, avoid peeling potatoes; just scrape them.

WHOLEMEAL (WHOLE WHEAT) BREAD
Nutritionists regard wholemeal bread as a staple protein food; if you team it with cheese or eggs, it makes one of the best packed sandwich lunches or snacks for growing teenagers, for instance. Small loaves are more expensive than large ones, and rolls or muffins are more expensive still. A home-made loaf, however, only costs about half as much as a bought loaf of the same size.

Home-made wholemeal (whole wheat) cakes and cookies are good value too.

WHOLEMEAL (WHOLE WHEAT) PASTA

Many shapes and sizes are now available, and they offer the same benefits (e.g. vitamins and minerals) as whole-grain breads. Cook them exactly like ordinary pasta of the same type but for a few minutes longer. Add the same sauces or other extras as to rice.

BROWN RICE

Brown rice costs more than white rice, but is worth it for the vitamins and minerals it contains, and for its nutty flavour. It also has a bit more protein. Team it with peas or beans, lentils or with small quantities of fish and some green leaf vegetables.

DRIED BEANS, LENTILS AND SPLIT PEAS (PULSES)

There are now many different kinds to choose from. They are best and usually cheapest if bought in bulk from an ethnic food store, because health food stores generally have higher overheads and smaller turnover. Supermarkets generally only carry a small choice. Any type of pulse is an excellent 'shelf' staple, and not all need long cooking. Split red lentils, for instance, do not need soaking at all, and cook in 20–40 minutes. Unlike other vegetables, cook pulses ahead of needing them, as the cooking time varies with how old they are. They swell a lot in cooking so 50 g/2 oz per person should be enough for a main dish.

SOAKING AND COOKING TIMES

	Soaking time in lukewarm water	Simmering time
Aduki beans	6 hours or overnight	$1\frac{1}{2}$–2 hours
Black-eyed beans	2–4 hours	45 minutes
Butter beans	overnight	2 hours
Chickpeas	overnight	3 hours
Haricot beans	overnight	$1\frac{1}{2}$–2 hours
Brown lentils	4 hours	1 hour
Red lentils	–	40 minutes or less
Mung beans	2–4 hours	20 minutes
Split peas (yellow or green)	–	$1\frac{1}{2}$ hours
Whole peas	4 hours	$1\frac{1}{2}$ hours
Pinto beans	2–4 hours	$1\frac{1}{2}$–2 hours
Red kidney beans	4 hours	$1\frac{1}{2}$–2 hours
Soya beans	overnight (in the refrigerator)	$3\frac{1}{2}$–4 hours (chill to cool)

If you live alone or only need a small quantity, canned beans are just as good to use as dried beans soaked and cooked at home, and the fuel you save may well compensate for the extra cost. Most common varieties of beans are sold in cans. A 425-g/15-oz can of beans contains about 250 g/ 9 oz drained cooked beans, and a 198-g/7½-oz can yields about 113 g/4 oz of drained cooked beans.

If you have a solid fuel stove which holds the heat overnight or some other means of cheap heating, and you can manage to cope with a fairly large heavy pan, dried beans or peas cooked 'from scratch' at home are, of course, more practical for a large family. (Make sure you boil red kidney beans well, for at least 15–20 minutes.) Combination cooking (page 81) may help you out with the cooking of these or other beans if the cooking time presents problems.

SOYA BEANS (SOYBEANS) AND SOYA PRODUCTS
Soya beans contain all the essential amino-acids, and contain nearly as much usable protein as meat (61 per cent compared with meat's 67 per cent). They are therefore an excellent staple food in any form. The only problem with whole soya beans is that they ferment easily, and must therefore be refrigerated or frozen, once cooked. However, they are well worth keeping in stock in the freezer if you have one.

The best known soya products with protein value in Britain are firm and soft (silken) tofu (low-calorie bean curd) sold in vacuum packs (firm) or in long-life cartons (silken), and TVP (textured vegetable protein). Soya milk is available in a good number of health-oriented food stores for strict vegetarians but it is not a complete substitute for whole cow's milk. Soya flour is also sold, and makes good quick breads and close-textured cakes and cookies if mixed with wheat flour.

Tofu, which is entirely flavourless and looks like firm junket, deserves to be better known. It can be flavoured and used in many different ways as a 'hidden' protein food; for instance 'silken' tofu can be processed with vegetables or fruit when puréeing them, to give the purée a creamy texture. If beaten into a sharp yoghurt, it makes the taste milder, and it can also be used to 'extend' a salad dressing.

TVP is a dried protein product, processed to look and 'chew' like meat. It is flavourless, although 'pseudo' meat flavours are given to the assorted shapes (chunks, strips, chiplets and 'mince') to make a substitute or 'extender' for meat. Being fairly cheap, it is a useful way to make a little meat go further if served in a well-flavoured sauce; 150 g/5 oz TVP when soaked makes up to the equivalent of 450 g/1 lb meat. It is included in a good many ready-to-use canned meat products for this reason. (Soya flour is included in certain makes of sausages and in commercially-made cakes and cookies as a cost-saver too.)

FISH

Except at the coast, fish is generally very little cheaper than meat, although it has many other merits. Oily fish supply vitamin D, needed to help us absorb the vital mineral, calcium, for instance, and the bones in canned sardines or salmon supply calcium itself. Fish also offers small amounts of other vitamins and minerals. White fish is low in fat, so ideal for slimmers. Any fish is extremely easy to eat if the bones are removed, so it is a valuable protein food for old people and small children.

CHICKEN

Once a luxury dish, chicken has become a cheap flesh meat, replacing veal as the 'carrier' for any number of sauces, and it is easy to cook in a great many different ways. Mass-produced, commercially-bred chickens, however, are generally rather fatty, with wads of solid fat around the vent and under the skin. Unless you remove the exposed fat (and preferably the skin) the flesh can be greasy (although doing so does mean that you get less weight for your money).

It is generally wasteful to buy chicken portions. The cost is high compared with that of a whole bird, which can also supply good stock (from the carcass). The cheapest way to buy chicken even for 1 or 2 people, if you have a refrigerator is to buy a whole boiling fowl – usually less fatty than a roasting chicken – and to skin and joint it yourself. There is often a surprising amount of good meat on the back of the carcass, which most people ignore.

Turkey is less fatty than chicken, and, although it is more expensive in most places and takes longer to cook, a single turkey portion may well be a better buy for two or three people than a chicken joint for each.

OFFAL OR VARIETY MEATS

Although some contain a lot of cholesterol (page 34), offal or variety meats such as liver, kidneys and heart are the cheapest forms of meats, and the richest in valuable vitamins and minerals. Ideally, one of them should feature in any low-budget diet for non-vegetarians at least once a week, on both counts. Unfortunately, however, many people are prejudiced against the idea of eating these meats, sometimes irrationally; a person who 'won't touch' liver, for instance, may happily eat liver sausage or chicken livers. In this and similar cases, recipes which mask the strong flavour of the unprocessed meat and hide its looks are worth searching for. Ox (beef) heart or small sheep's hearts also arouse a reaction of distaste, although both provide good muscle meat if cooked slowly in a casserole; a stuffed sheep's heart has the particular virtue of being the right size to make a meal for one person, when the excess fat and any tubes and inner membranes have been removed.

Variety meats from beef are generally the cheapest, although the strongest-tasting and coarsest. Any kind needs slow cooking, say braising rather than grilling. Pigs' organ or variety meats are also cheap and strong-tasting, so need handling the same way. Small lambs' offal meats are much more delicate (and costly), while calves' offal is generally a luxury dish.

Ox (beef) tongue is also generally acceptable despite the fact that it is distinctly fatty, *and* needs long cooking; yet small sheep's tongues, which each make a good meal for one person and which cook relatively quickly, usually get the 'thumbs down' sign (probably because they are more nuisance to skin).

SAUSAGES AND 'BURGERS
Neither of these processed products is cheap to buy ready made, and the amount of fat in any sausage is perilously high. Good, cheap, and nourishing 'burgers are, however, very easy to make at home. It is worth buying good-quality lean mince (ground beef) for them; the cost can be reduced by mixing in wholemeal (whole wheat) breadcrumbs, a little soya flour or potato, finely chopped nuts, fresh chopped herbs etc. You will find several variations on the usual meat 'burgers in the recipe section.

NUTS
By far the cheapest nuts, and the best for protein value, are raw, unsalted peanuts. Almonds have about two-thirds as much protein, but are much more expensive. Brazils, walnuts and hazelnuts contain slightly less protein than almonds.

Shelled nuts are almost the same price as unshelled nuts, but blanched skinned nuts are a lot more expensive, so it is well worth while blanching and skinning them at home. They can be chopped in a food processor or coffee-grinder (take care not to over-process them or they will 'oil'). Chopped nuts are an excellent food to add to croquette mixtures, salads and stews, or to the topping for a sweet crumble or (home-made) ice cream.

3. CARBOHYDRATES

Carbohydrates are not what you may think. To many people they mean sugary and starchy refined foods which make us fat without serving any useful purpose. Carbohydrates as a whole are almost the opposite of that.

Carbohydrates, in fact, are as essential to life, in their way, as proteins, because they supply most of the energy or 'power' which makes the body's mechanisms function. They almost all come from plant foods, and the energy they supply has been obtained from sunlight and stored in the plants. Carbohydrates are also the storage containers of some of the essential vitamins and minerals, which we can only get hold of to use by eating plant foods.

It is true that carbohydrates are sugars and starches, but it is important to distinguish between the ones we cannot afford to do without and those which will be harmful if we eat too much of them.

SUGARS AND STARCHES

There are two main groups of carbohydrates: simple and double sugars (called by scientists *saccharides* and *disaccharides*), and the complex carbohydrates called *polysaccharides*. (Notice these names in case you see them on can labels.) Here are some notes about the important ones in each group.

SIMPLE SUGARS

Glucose sweets are well-known as a quick energy-booster; and powdered glucose is an easily-digested form of sugar given to invalids because it gets into the bloodstream quickly, to keep up their blood sugar level. All energy-producing carbohydrates are changed into simple sugars, mainly glucose, when we digest them, either for quick use or for storage. We get some natural glucose from ripe fruit, and – oddly – from onions, along with traces of other nutrients.

Fructose (which is very like glucose) occurs in fruit and fruit juices, and also in honey.

DOUBLE SUGARS

Sucrose (mainly from sugar cane and beet juice) and lactose (milk sugar) are the commonest double sugars. The sugar cane and beet plants, when processed, provide all the pure refined white and brown sugars, such as granulated sugar, icing (confectioner's) sugar and demerara (brown crystal) sugar.

COMPLEX SUGARS

The most fascinating carbohydrate is starch, because it is the food store of the living plants and of the seeds, tubers and roots from which new plants will grow. In these embryo plants, it comes 'packaged' with every kind of nutrient which the new plant needs for life and growth; good protein, vitamins and minerals as well as the (polysaccharide) carbohydrate. So when we eat bread, beans or potatoes, we get a wonderful 'package deal' of vital, life-supportive nutrients – provided we make sure that we eat the part of the 'package' which contains them, such as the 'germ' and outer layers of a wheat grain or the layer just underneath the skin of a potato.

We get something else too. The 'package' also includes the complicated carbohydrate called cellulose or, more often, fibre, which makes up the structure of plants; human beings cannot fully digest it but it has come to be thought so important for our positive health and well-being that I have given the whole of Chapter 6 to it.

Looking at this list of carbohydrates, which do you think offer you the best value? It is obvious, really, that a 'package' including good protein back-up, varied vitamins and fibre as well, has merits over merely sugar alone.

The only thing starchy foods lack is sweetness; but our sweet tooth as well as our need for quick energy sometimes can largely be catered for by fruits, and especially by the concentrated sweetness of dried fruits. Raw fresh and dried fruits offer simple sugars (glucose and fructose) together with sun-gathered vitamins and minerals, and with fibre in their flesh and skins.

THE COST OF SWEETNESS

Both seasonal and imported *fresh fruits* can fluctuate in price unnervingly, wherever you live. Some steady old world-wide favourites, however, are available year-round and usually quite cheaply from some source. Apples are one of our sweetest and best as well as one of our cheapest fresh fruits, although dessert pears come close behind. There are, literally, hundreds of ways of using both, in savoury as well as sweet dishes, and in cakes: look for instance, at the recipes for Grilled (Broiled) Mackerel with Nuts and Apples*, Oatmeal Apple Crumble*, or Baked Apples filled with Raisins* (with a spoonful of honey on top for a treat).

Granted, *dried fruits* are expensive but their concentrated sweetening value is so high that you only need a few in most dishes. More than half the weight of sultanas or dried figs consists of calcium-rich carbohydrate.

Honey has always been a treat food, too expensive for ordinary people to use every day. It is often said that honey is no better for health than white sugar because it only contains marginal traces of nutrients other than sugars, and no fibre at all. However, if you take into account the fact that the lovely flavour of honey makes it *seem* sweeter than white sugar, you may feel justified in buying an occasional pot for a feast, although you should remember that wholefruit jam or marmalade are better buys as sweeteners nutrients-wise (they are better still if home-made, from fresh whole fruit). They are also, of course much cheaper.

Syrups, such as treacle (molasses) or maple syrup are also much cheaper flavourings than honey, although they, too, cost more than white sugar.

In some ways, we are not tempted to use syrup or a sweet preserve as often or as regularly as white sugar. You would not sweeten your coffee or tea with treacle or jam, for instance. But the particular risk which both sugar and syrups present to our pockets and, more seriously, to our health, is that, unless we are alert, we so easily get addicted to eating regularly far more foods heavily sweetened with sucrose (double sugar) than we need; and on top of these we get still more sugar in hidden and semi-hidden ways which we may hardly notice are sweet but which surreptitiously please our sweet tooth.

One way to find out how many of your daily foods contain sugar is to look at the ingredients lists given on cans and packages, and at the order in which the ingredients are listed. They are given in descending order of quantity. If the list has sugar or one of its scientific names (monosaccharide or disaccharide) among the first few ingredients, put that can or package back on the shelf; it is heavy with sugar.

Many breakfast cereals contain a good deal of sugar, and most people sprinkle on still more. Canned fruits in syrup are obviously soaked in sugar; but it is also used as a preservative and hidden flavouring in many canned and frozen ready-to-serve meals, in sausages and in canned meats and vegetables. Then what about cakes and biscuits, ice creams (and toppings), squashes and bottled soft drinks, chocolate bars and a night-time sweet drink? If you add up just the sugar you consume between meals, almost without realising it, the cost can be high. So is the cost in clothes and confidence if you put on weight.

THE FATNESS FACTOR

Plain white sugar is an insidious fattener, even when you know you are eating it, because it lacks bulk; so is brown sugar. You do not have to chew it, and so activate your salivary glands and other digestive juices, nor do you get the comfortable feeling of eating solid food; so your appetite control mechanism does not get alerted properly, and the sugar slips into your bloodstream without you realising how many calories' worth of meringues or ice cream you have taken in.

When you digest sugary or starchy food, your digestive juices break it down into glucose (simple sugar), and it goes through your intestine walls into your bloodstream, (where we call it blood sugar). This blood sugar passes to all parts of your body to keep it 'ticking over' efficiently, and as heat. Just a little is stored for quick emergency use in your muscles and liver. Your bloodstream never holds more blood sugar than it needs at once, so any blood sugar which it cannot use or store at once it dumps as fat in different parts of your body, either temporarily or (too often) permanently.

When you eat sweets or other sugary foods which consist almost entirely of carbohydrate, you may easily get a lot of sugar in your bloodstream which has no work to do and so gets 'parked' as fat.

Many people ask 'Aren't starchy foods as fattening as sugary ones?' The simple answer is 'Yes', if you eat too much of them; but this is less likely to happen than in the case of sugary foods.

First, it depends partly on what you use the starchy food for. For instance, if you have Eggs in Potato Nests* or a beefburger in a bun for supper, you are using the dish to supply your protein as well as the energy in the carbohydrate; the egg or 'burger will help to make you feel well-fed without an extra (sweet) bun or cake.

The second thing on which the risk of taking too much starchy carbohydrate depends is what *kind* of starch you eat. Whole-grain foods and pulses have important hidden merits for slenderness and health.

First, you tend to digest them more slowly than either refined starchy or sugary foods; your digestive system breaks them down more slowly

27

into glucose (simple sugar) and releases it into your bloodstream slowly, not in a 'burst' of more sugar than you will need all at once. (The main reason why you digest these grains and pulses more slowly is that they come in a 'package' with dietary fibre [Chapter 6] which your digestive system has to untangle before it can break down the carbohydrate into simple sugar.)

Another merit of these foods is that their fibrous bulk, texture and satisfying nutty flavour tend to make them seem more filling than refined starchy or sugary foods; so you tend to need less of them to feel pleasantly well-fed. This may slightly reduce the calories you take in. Also slightly less of their total calorie value is absorbed into your body than in the case of refined starches and sugars. The extra goes out with the undigested fibre.

THE HEALTH FACTOR

Starch, not sugar, has always been mankind's main source of food energy, simply because it has always been the chief energy store of most plants. In fact we would hardly have any sugar in our diet at all except milk sugar and fructose from fruit and honey if we had not learned to use the processed sucrose in cane and beet sugar. So becoming addicted to sugar is unnatural, and, like most kinds of addiction, is likely to be bad for our health.

This idea is supported by what we know about people's diet in the past. We know that late Stone Age people had teeth ground down by hard chewing but little or no signs of tooth decay. Whole grains were their staple foods, and fruits their main sweetener. In fact, starches, especially whole grains were the staple food and dried fruits were the sweetener of all ordinary folk until quite recent times. They died young of many diseases, but, to judge by people who still live on the same foods, heart disease, strokes, diabetes, bowel cancer and other bowel diseases were not among them. These are modern 'killer' diseases.

White bread is the commonest Western staple today. It lacks many of the virtues of whole-grain bread, but is has certain merits of its own. For one thing, it is often fortified (in some places by law) with valuable 'extras' in the form of vitamins (see page 38) and calcium (page 51). Potatoes with their skins on contain valuable nutrients too. It is an excess of the single and double sugars without any other nutrients which seems to do such fatal damage.

We know today that too much sugar and too many sweets, especially between meals, also play a part in causing tooth decay. Besides this, many scientists are now convinced that too much sugar can contribute to making us perilously overweight, which strains the heart. It also makes our organs overwork in spasms to cope with sudden rushes of sugar (which may just get stored as fat). Besides this, it is so sweet and easy to eat that we easily become addicted to it without knowing it.

HOW MUCH IS TOO MUCH?

Notice that I have said 'too much sugar' in the previous paragraph; I have not suggested that all refined sugar is harmful all the time, any more than white bread. In fact we all need a quick burst of energy sometimes, say when spring-cleaning or running for a bus. Men who do sudden hard physical work, such as firemen, and school-kids who play team ball games need a lot more quick energy intermittently than most of us. A housewife also probably really needs that cup of tea with sugar in the middle of a hard wash-day. What we should all cut down on, for safety's sake, if no more, is our regular consumption of sugar 'in more or less everything'.

Even a hundred years ago, the proportion of starch to sugar, eaten mostly as bread, porridge and potatoes, was much higher than it is today. We cannot lay down hard-and-fast rules for the 'right' proportion of starch to sugar to eat, because everyone's needs vary. But the number of people who die young from the modern 'killer' diseases shows that the quantity of sugar we eat regularly is much too high.

MAKING CHANGES

Pleasant bad habits are not easy to break, but this one should be easier than most because it need not mean rigid self-denial. There is no need to cut out all sugar; not only do we all need some occasionally, we all need a modest treat sometimes too. A spoonful of sugar or dab of jam is a cheap one. We need not leave large gaps in the pattern of foods we usually eat (and drink) either. As a rule we can substitute other foods or drinks of a similar type. If you strike problems, introduce changes slowly, and get used to one at a time.

Sugar is insidiously cheap, so some of the new foods will cost more in money as well as in work. Home-made sweets made with dried fruits are delicious but cost more than sherbet lemons from a store. It is more trouble to make snacks using 'wise' ingredients and to persuade the kids to try them than to buy ones from the supermarket shelf which they already like. If you are elderly and live alone, it may be hard to give up sweet cakes over a chat with a friend. Only you can decide whether it is worth it.

Below are some ideas to help you. First, turn to Table 2 in Appendix II showing the proportions of sugar and starch which some common foods contain. Make a note of the sugary ones, so that you can cut down on them. Then read the paragraphs below which contain ideas for substitutes you may like to use.

Notice, in particular, that you can often compensate for the reduced sugar by substituting extra starch. For instance, if you substituted canned peaches in water or natural juice for peaches in syrup as a dessert, sprinkle them with Home-Made Muesli 'Mix'* or Digestive Biscuit (Granola Cracker) crumbs.

Using starchy foods will help to compensate for the extra cost of dried fruit and other healthy 'goodies'. Remember, it is poor people who, through the ages, have relied on starchy foods such as whole-grain flour and seeds for both their protein and energy for whom bread really has been 'the staff of life'.

There are quite a lot of ways in which you can reduce the proportion of sugary foods which you eat without feeling deprived. For instance, try these ideas:

1) Substitute foods containing some whole-grain or vegetable starch for ones containing only white starch and a lot of sugar, e.g. Carrot Cake* for a melt-in-the-mouth sponge cake.

2) Substitute savoury snacks and other foods for sweet ones whenever you can, e.g. choose a packet of unsalted peanuts to nibble instead of sweet popcorn.

3) Substitute your own, less sugary versions of salad dressings and sauces for bought ones (or use low-sugar, low-calorie ones if you cannot make your own).

4) Substitute straight non-sugary drinks, e.g. fresh unsweetened orange juice for orange squash.

5) EAT LESS SUGAR GENERALLY. For instance:

a) Try to get used to tea and coffee without sugar, and avoid colas and other fizzy drinks like the plague; they are dangerous because you can drink them so quickly, and they are loaded with sugar; if you must have them, drink the low-sugar, 'low-cal' kinds.

b) Use a bit less sugar than the recipes call for if you make your own desserts, cakes, and similar goodies, and give them fruit toppings and fillings instead of icing. If you are not into baking, buy whole wheat, rolled-oat or branny kinds – there are some in most supermarkets.

30

c) Stew fruit with little or no sugar; you will be surprised how soon you get used to it.

d) Try making your own minced fruit preserves if you can; they are excellent, and add a little extra vitamin C to your diet. Otherwise, try to buy one at a health food shop sometimes – yes, they ARE pricey but they spread very thinly and go a long way.

6) AVOID SUGARY FOODS WHEN YOU SHOP. Besides the ones mentioned above, walk straight past the shelves holding:

a) sugary breakfast cereals (Home-Made Muesli 'Mix'* is cheaper);

b) cream-filled, sugar-coated and chocolate biscuits;

c) canned fruits in heavy syrup – fruits canned in natural juice are tastier than ones canned in water, and not expensive;

d) instant packet soups, sauces and desserts, canned puddings and canned meats (unless you 'clear' the label first, see p.72), as many of these contain sugar;

e) frozen and freeze-dried ready-to-use meals – again unless you 'clear' the label; these, too, are often loaded with sugar and other 'nasties' and they are usually expensive as well.

This may seem like a long list of 'Don'ts' – but remember that it is not a rigid one. Mostly, it is suggesting cutting down, not cutting out. You are entitled to treats sometimes; just keep them modest. After all, one glacé cherry on your sundae looks as good as two!

Hopefully, you will soon stop noticing that you are eating less sugar. If you still do, just add up how much you *have not* spent on sweets or gooey slices of gâteau this week – and how many unwanted calories *are not* sitting on your hips as a result.

4. FATS AND OILS

Fat protects your health in certain important ways. First, some vital vitamins (A, D, E and K), called fat-soluble vitamins, are almost only found in fatty and oily foods. If you try to do without fats and oils entirely, you may risk going short of one of these vitamins. Doctors also think that we cannot keep really well without the components of fats called essential fatty acids. Fatty acids help to make up fats in much the same way as amino-acids make up proteins; essential fatty acids, which are found largely in vegetable oils, are ones which we cannot make in our own bodies.

Fat also, quite literally, protects you, because everyone in normal health has a layer of fat under the skin and around the kidneys and some other organs to protect them from damage. The fatty layer under your skin helps to keep you warm inside – rather like the insulation round a hot-water tank – keeping in the heat which you get from eating food.

Since you cannot do without the fat-soluble vitamins and essential fatty acids, and certainly need a protective layer of fat, even slimmers *must* eat SOME fat.

However, fat is a concentrated source of energy, supplying twice as many calories, weight for weight, as carbohydrate (or 9 calories per gram of fat). It is also an easy (some of us would say too easy) form of storage for 'dumping' excess energy from fatty foods as well as from unused carbohydrates. For these reasons, eating too much fat is the quickest way to GET fat, which is certainly bad for your health.

Eating too much fat may also hold other risks for your health. To find out what these are, we need to know what fats are made of, and which are the most sensible kinds to eat to make our food pleasant without eating too much.

WHAT ARE FATS AND OILS MADE OF?

Basically, oils are fats which are liquid at normal temperatures. There are a great many different fats and oils, just as there are different proteins and carbohydrates. They are all, however, mixtures made largely of the fatty acids mentioned above, and the make-up of each fat or oil varies according to the number, quantity and types of fatty acids in its own particular 'mix'. Fatty acids are generally divided into three types according to their molecular make-up, namely:

1) saturated fatty acids;
2) monounsaturated fatty acids;
3) polyunsaturated fatty acids.

Most fats and oils contain both saturated and unsaturated fatty acids. On the whole, those with a high proportion of saturated fatty acids make solid fats such as butter, while those with a lot more unsaturated fatty acids make oils such as olive oil (monounsaturated) and corn oil (polyunsaturated).

We get food fats from both animals and plants, and both are usually 'packaged' with fat-soluble vitamins. Animal fats may contain vitamin A and vitamin D. Some vegetable fats contain carotene (which your body can turn into vitamin A) and vitamin E.

We get most of our animal fats from:
1) milk and milk products, e.g. butter, cream and cheese;
2) meat fats, e.g. lard, suet and solid fat in the flesh and under the skin;
3) egg yolk;
4) fatty fish and fish liver oils.

Except for fish fats and oils, most of these fats contain a lot more saturated fatty acids than unsaturated ones.

Plants make their fats from their carbohydrate stores as they age and ripen; peanuts, coconuts and soya beans may contain 20–40 per cent oil when ripe. Our vegetable food fats come mainly from:

1) nuts, e.g. peanut butter, groundnut (peanut) oil;
2) seeds, e.g. sunflower oil, corn oil;
3) fruits, e.g. olive oil, avocado oil;
4) margarines made from vegetable fats and oils.
NB Margarines labelled 'high in polyunsaturated fats' usually contain some saturated fats as well. Check the list of ingredients before you buy.

Coconuts and cashew nuts are popular foods high in saturated fatty acids. But most other vegetable fats and oils contain mainly polyunsaturated fatty acids.

HOW MUCH FAT DO WE EAT?

Nearly all the visible fats we eat, such as butter, cream, bacon and chicken fat, are animal fats high in saturated fatty acids; only peanut butter and certain margarines and cooking fats made from vegetable oils are exceptions. Most of us therefore eat some animal fats every day, as spreads on our breads, with desserts or when we eat meats or fried foods.

However, these are not the only fats we eat. In fact, they only supply about half our fat intake. The rest is tucked away in meat (especially pig meat), in fatty fish, in pastry, puddings and cakes, ice cream, sauces and so on. Even if we cut every morsel of visible fat out of our meals, we would still be eating a good deal of fat – quite a lot of it high in saturated fatty acids.

Table 3 in Appendix II compares the average quantity of fat in various foods. Remember that, in a lot of foods, the quantity may vary widely, for instance with the particular cut of meat or package of nuts which you eat, or with the season. Herrings, for instance, may contain 10–25 per cent fat depending on the time of year.

HOW MUCH FAT SHOULD WE EAT, AND WHAT KIND?

Authorities agree that most of us eat too much fat. Obesity, especially in children, is becoming a serious problem and it can make us vulnerable to many ills sooner or later. But even being slightly overweight is now thought to be risky. Why?

One reason is that the diseases known as diabetes and high blood pressure are both associated with being overweight, and the risks seem to get greater the more excess weight one puts on. People who suffer or who seem at risk from either disease are therefore often told to get their weight down among other things. Cutting down their intake of fats, especially those rich in saturated fatty acids, is one of the important ways in which they are told to slim down.

Although high blood pressure is widely discussed because it can lead to coronary heart disease, other diseases such as atherosclerosis ('hardening of the arteries') may also be more serious if we are overweight, especially as we get older. We should all, therefore, cut down our total consumption of fats, and use as the fats we need (see page 32) fats high in poly-unsaturated fatty acids.

This is partly because a high intake of saturated fatty acids is thought to increase the amount of the fat-like substance called *cholesterol* in our blood. Cholesterol is found in all animal foods, especially those containing saturated fatty acids, but it does not occur in plant foods.

Since our bodies, like those of all animals, make cholesterol anyway, we do not need a lot extra from our diet; in fact excess cholesterol is thought to be linked with atherosclerosis and heart disease along with other factors including, notably, stress, lack of exercise and smoking. It is important to cope with all these problems for your general health's sake. Cutting down on foods which are high in cholesterol and saturated fatty acids may be one of the easier solutions to find.

HOW TO CUT DOWN ON FATS

1) One easy and indeed obvious way to cut down on the quantities of fats you use is to turn over to using oil for frying and grilling (broiling). Strictly speaking, you should avoid fried foods altogether, but it may be difficult just to give them up completely. Using oil may take a bit of getting used to, but it is worthwhile; it gives you deliciously crisp products – and remember that it is a good deal cheaper than solid fat as well as more efficient. Oil spreads further, faster, so you use less of it. It also burns less easily than animal fats.

If you really want to fry foods, try to invest in a non-stick pan in which you can 'dry fry' with very little or no oil. If possible, get a deep one in which you can also stir-fry foods occasionally for quick, cheap, excellent vegetable meals – just 2 tablespoonfuls of oil will stir-fry a whole dish for four to six people. Use one of the polyunsaturated oils in the list above.

With a little practice, you will soon find that you can make appetising meals with much less fat than you have been used to, or even with none at all. Vegetables taste deliciously fresh if steamed or short-cooked in stock rather than being boiled in water and then doused in fat. Scrambled or poached eggs are just as good as fried eggs, and need a lot less fat, or none at all.

2) Choose lean meats if you eat flesh foods and cut off the visible fat before you cook them. 'Pot-roast' a joint, if you have one, without extra fat, just with a little stock or water in the pot; it will be partly steamed and succulent (this is a good, tenderising method for all cheaper cuts). Try to substitute chicken or fish for red meats, especially the fattier meats such as pork, whenever you can. Modern chickens are also quite fatty, so take any wads of fat out of the vent end before cooking. It is really sensible to remove the skin too.

3) In theory, you should avoid eating many eggs because the yolk contains a quite startlingly high quantity of cholesterol. But they are cheap, and are convenient and quick to cook. They are also very easy for elderly people and small children to digest. It would therefore be a pity to

cut them out entirely although it is a good idea to limit them to three or four a week per person. Use them at intervals; do not make for instance a main dish of scrambled eggs followed by a baked custard for supper. When you do serve scrambled (or other) eggs, use only one egg per person, and add a 'filler' such as grilled tomato halves or aubergine slices. Keep an eye, too, on the 'hidden' eggs you use. Savoury pancakes use fewer eggs than omelets (and need no more fat). Choose cakes and cookies with few or no eggs when you can. Honey Cinnamon Squares* are an example.

4) Avoid fat-based sauces and dressing for salads. Mayonnaise is your enemy. Yoghurt-based dressings can be delicious; try mixing a little tofu (page 21) if you can afford it (from a health food store). As for 'cream' sauces, some of the best high-class cooks substitute a simple vegetable purée, just with a light seasoning and a few chopped fresh herbs. Vegetable and fruit juices also make good cheap bases for sauces.

5) When you want baked goods, remember the merits of savoury and sweet tea breads and scones (biscuits) compared with fat-loaded cakes. Scones (biscuits) make good shortcake-style desserts. Some pastry goods contain less fat than cakes, but avoid the rich pastries such as puff pastry, flaky pastry and suet crust (boiled crust) pastry. Many people do not like cakes and cookies made with oil, but use it if you do not mind the flavour.

IS IT EXPENSIVE TO CHANGE?

No. It will cost you less if anything to use mostly polyunsaturated fats. Here are some of the ways in which it should save you money.

1) *Main dish protein foods*. Vegetable protein foods are cheaper than animal foods on the whole. Risotto, pasta or a savoury bean stew costs less than a similar meat or fish dish. Any frying needed in cooking them can be done with oil, as it is in the countries these dishes come from.

You will also win on costs by choosing animal protein foods with polyunsaturated fats. Mackerel, herring and sardines are among the cheaper fish, and contain both plenty of vitamin D which you cannot get from plant foods and calcium as well; you do not *have to* choose salmon. Chicken is usually a lot cheaper than red meat, and also has the virtue of being rich in chromium.

2) *Fats and oils*. When you choose your oil, buying the cheapest blended oil may be false economy healthwise unless the label specifies that it only contains vegetable oils; as a rule it is wiser to spend a little more and buy an oil labelled as a pure vegetable oil, preferably one in the list on page 33 above. Choose one light oil for all purposes; you pay for each bottle as

well as the contents. Do not be beguiled into buying olive oil. Its cost is high and it is generally less stable for frying than a lighter oil, as well as less adaptable for other cooking. On a tight budget, it is frankly an unnecessary luxury. (Use spicy and herb salad dressings for flavour).

As for solid fat, you obviously gain pricewise by using margarine instead of butter. Do read the label on the pack before you buy, though, and make sure it specifies that the fat is made from polyunsaturated fats alone. You may have to pay a bit more for it than for a blended margarine, but, if possible, grit your teeth and do it.

3) Lastly, here is a good health rule which will also save you a bit of money. Never serve a fatty food alone. You may risk a bilious attack or headache (especially if you are elderly or tend to have stomach upsets). Supply your body with carbohydrate for energy at the same time. This carbohydrate will bulk out, and so reduce, the quantity of fatty food you eat. So there is food sense as well as pocket sense in serving whole-grain bread with cheese or 'mash' (creamed potato) with the single sausage you may have as a treat.

5. VITAMINS AND MINERALS

VITAMINS

Vitamins are like the fuses in your body's power circuit. Each of them sets in motion or regulates certain processes in your body which are vital for healthy living.

On a normal Western diet, you are never likely to be *wholly* deprived of most vitamins, but it is quite easy to go short of one or more of them, by failing to eat enough foods which contain them, or by cooking them carelessly. Then your body's processes will work feebly, rather like a flickering light or power circuit, and you will be less well and active than you could be otherwise. This wastes both the nutrients you eat and your body's capacity for vigour and enjoyment. It's a needless waste, too, because it's just as cheap and easy to choose the right foods for maximum vitamin intake and to prepare them properly as not.

This section covers, first, the jobs which the various vitamins do, and what happens if your body lacks one or more of them. Then there are suggestions for ways to make sure you get enough of each.

TWO TYPES OF VITAMINS

There are two kinds of vitamins: ones which dissolve in fat, and ones which dissolve in water. Your body stores the fat-soluble ones (A, D, E and K) if they are not used, but almost entirely throws out the unused water-soluble ones (the various B vitamins and vitamin C).

HOW MUCH OF EACH DO WE NEED?

You need to take in enough of each vitamin to keep you not just ticking over but at your own peak level. However, everyone varies as to just how much of each vitamin he or she needs; and, in any case, the quantity of each is so small and may vary so much in most types of food that it would be almost impossible to measure it. The wisest course, therefore, is to make sure that you take in a supply regularly, and that it is not destroyed by poor or careless cooking before it reaches your plate.

Make sure, in particular, that you get some B vitamins and vitamin C every day; it is extremely difficult to get too much. You need not worry if your intake of A, D, E and K varies quite a lot over four or five days; you will have a reserve supply. *Do not*, however, go on a wild crank diet and eat, for instance, nothing but carrots for a week, or load yourself up with vitamin pills; an excess of stored fat-soluble vitamins might then do you harm, although it will not happen on a normal Western diet.

THE COOK'S SIMPLE GUIDE TO VITAMINS

Fat-soluble Vitamins	*Low-cost Foods which Contain Them*
VITAMIN A is sometimes called *retinol*. You can only get it from animal foods; but vegetable foods and milk give you *carotenes* which your body can change into retinol. Labels on bottles and cans sometimes refer to *retinol equivalents* to describe the total quantity of vitamin A energy you get to use. *What Vitamin A does:* 1) It helps to protect you from infection, especially of the skin and the mucus membranes inside your body. 2) It can strengthen your sight, especially in dim light. *Tip:* Do not throw away the coarse outside leaves of cabbage, spring greens or spinach, or the green tops of leeks. Shred them for soup or stir-fries (see page 35). The outer leaves of green vegetables gain carotenes from sunshine as they get older and darker in colour.	Liver, kidneys, cheese, eggs, milk, herrings, fish liver oils. Margarine (with vitamins added). Dark green vegetables, such as cabbage, spinach, watercress, kale. Carrots, turnip tops, tomatoes. Dried apricots, prunes.

VITAMIN D is made by our bodies from sunlight. This is much the best way to get it, although you can get a bit second-hand by eating animal foods, and it is easily and simply made artificially from plants (the form used for supplements and additions to foods).

Most people get quite enough vitamin D from sunlight, but certain groups of people need an extra supply, especially in winter when there is less sunlight for both humans and animals to use.

Make sure that anyone you care for in these groups (including yourself) gets enough vitamin D:

1) people living in the far north, and those who are housebound, e.g. invalids or elderly people;

2) people who wear cover-up clothes always, such as some Asian women;

3) women who are pregnant or breast-feeding a baby; all growing children.

What vitamin D does:

Together with calcium and phosphorus (pages 51 and 52), vitamin D builds strong bones and teeth, beginning before a baby is born. If a pregnant mother or growing child does not get enough vitamin D, the child's bones may be too weak to support it, and the disease called rickets can result. The child may then be bow-legged and knock-kneed for life.

Canned or processed fatty fish, e.g. tuna, herring, mackerel, sardines, cod liver oil.
Evaporated milk, margarine (with vitamins added).
Eggs, liver, Cheddar or similar cheese.

Another risk for some people is bone-softening. Teenagers who are growing fast are at risk and so are mothers who repeatedly become pregnant while still breast-feeding their babies. Oid people may also suffer. This is because they absorb too little calcium; their life-style and diet let them go short of it, or of vitamin D its team-mate.

Yet another risk for anyone short of vitamin D is badly formed teeth.

Tips: (Under Britain's National Health Service, pregnant and nursing mothers and the under-fives can get supplements including vitamin D which are free for those who cannot afford to buy them.) A free form of self-help is to make sure you take a walk or sit outside for half an hour every day when the weather lets you. Eat cheese on toast or canned fatty fish (including the bones) about once a week. Give children a coleslaw with Milk Salad Dressing* sometimes.

VITAMIN E was claimed as a wonderful fertility booster when it was first discovered, but without proof. Its main role was not clear when this book was published but it is associated with how your body uses polyunsaturated fats (page 33). It is almost impossible to get too little.

Tip: Do not worry about it. If you stick to a sensible, whole-grain based diet, you have got it.

Most foods, especially vegetable oils, whole-grain cereals and eggs.

41

Fat-soluble Vitamins	Low-cost Foods which Contain Them
VITAMIN K is needed for normal blood clotting. You will not go short because your body can make it, and it occurs in many vegetable foods. *Tip:* Relax, and forget about it.	Cabbage, cauliflower, spinach and other green leafy vegetables. Ox (beef) liver.

Water-soluble B Vitamins and Vitamin C	Low-cost Foods which Contain Them
ALL B VITAMINS have three things in common. 1) They act together to make the energy you get from all your food work in your body. 2) They are easily lost in cooking water (especially with an alkali such as baking soda) and they are destroyed by high heat. 3) Your body throws out any it does not use almost at once. This means that, unless you keep taking them in regularly, you are likely to be short of several, not just one. So, if your diet were to become gravely inadequate, you might, quite soon, suffer from symptoms of several serious 'deficiency' diseases at the same time.	
THIAMINE (vitamin B_1) frees the energy you get from carbohydrates so you need enough thiamine to cope with *all* the carbohydrate you eat. In several countries, white bread is fortified to replace the thiamine removed with the wheat germ when the flour is milled, either by law as in	Yeast, fortified white bread, and breakfast cereals, oatmeal, wholemeal (whole wheat) bread and pasta, brown rice, roasted peanuts, fresh green peas, beans, potatoes, liver, kidneys, pork belly (bacon piece), other meats (a little), eggs.

Britain, or voluntarily by millers as in the USA.

Refined foods such as polished white rice, fats and sugar contain no thiamine, and it is easily lost from any food which is not carefully cooked. You may lose up to 25 per cent of the thiamine in raw foods in cooking water, for instance, or more if you use an alkali such as baking soda. High heat in pressure cooking destroys it too.

Tips: Simmer vegetables in very little water, and always without soda; keep cooking water for soups and sauces. Always use the pan juices and drippings from any roast to make gravy or soup, too. Use oatmeal for coating grilled foods such as 'burgers or fish. Stick to whole-grain, yeast-raised bread, brown rice and pasta.

NOTE Preserved meats such as corned beef and sausages contain very little thiamine.

RIBOFLAVIN (vitamin B$_2$) is vital because you cannot use the energy you get from food without it. It occurs in a lot of foods in small quantities, but it is destroyed by light and by high heat, and also gets lost (like thiamine) in cooking water and meat drippings or when you cook with an alkali such as baking soda.

Lack of riboflavin can cause mouth sores, a poor skin, and make you depressed, and it may check a child's growth. However, it occurs in so many foods that you are very unlikely ever to go short of it.

Yeast, liver and kidneys, eggs, whole-grain and fortified cereals, milk and milk products, pulses.

43

Tip: Do not leave the milk bottle on the doorstep. If you bake cakes, make the family an old-fashioned yeast cake or sweet yeast-raised tea bread sometimes.

NICOTINIC ACID (NIACIN) is another B vitamin which shares the job of turning food energy to good use. One form of it occurs naturally in your body; but your body also makes nicotinic acid (niacin) from foods which contain an amino-acid called tryptophan. So, just as with vitamin A, we can measure the quantity of usable nicotinic acid you get in *units* of *nicotinic acid equivalent*.

Animal protein foods and fish, dairy foods and – strangely – instant coffee provide tryptophan generously; peas, and wholemeal (whole wheat) bread provide plenty too. So no one on a varied western diet should go short.

Tip: Make sure of your proteins and your nicotinic acid supply will be secure.

Chicken meat, liver and kidneys, yeast, eggs, whole-grain bread and other whole-grain cereals, peas and dried beans.

PYRIDOXINE (vitamin B_6) helps your body to make use of the amino-acids in your food proteins, so the amount you need depends on how much protein you eat. But your body also needs it to make haemoglobin, the red material in your blood, which carries oxygen to every tissue in your body; you cannot live without it.

Cheaper kinds of meat and fish, eggs, whole-grain bread and other whole-grain cereals, green vegetables, peanuts, bananas.

Pyridoxine is part of the vitamin 'package' in many foods, and most people get an ample supply if they eat sensibly. If you are on 'the pill' or pregnant, it may be a good idea to eat a bit extra of the protein foods which contain it.

Tip: A slice or two of liver sausage need not be expensive to buy, and it is easy to eat, just as it is or toasted on whole-grain bread under the grill (in the broiler pan).

VITAMIN B_{12} is needed by the busiest cells in your body, the ones which make blood. It is the only vitamin you cannot get from any vegetable food, so if you are a vegan (a person who eats no animal food or product, not even milk), you may go short of it. In this case, you should take a special supplement, to save yourself from getting pernicious anaemia.

Liver, especially ox (beef) liver, white and some canned fatty fish, egg yolks, cheese and milk.

If you are a vegetarian, who eats animal products such as milk and eggs but not flesh foods, make sure you include enough of them in your meals.

Tip: Do not skip animal proteins because you are too busy to eat, or as a slimming gimmick. Eat a piece of low-fat hard cheese at the bus-stop or a skim-milk yoghurt instead of mid-morning coffee, if no more.

FOLIC ACID works with vitamin B_{12} and if you do not get enough of it you may, again, risk suffering from anaemia (a different kind from pernicious anaemia). If you are active and eat sensibly, you certainly will not be short of it because you will get good supplies in several different foods; look at the list on the right! However, folic acid gets 'lost' very easily when cooking vegetables in water, and you do not always digest all you eat, so make sure you take in plenty. If you are pregnant, you need extra.

Liver, raw leafy green vegetables, dried peas and beans, whole wheat bread.

Getting enough folic acid can be a real problem for the elderly people with small appetites, who may not bother to eat properly because they are not hungry.

Tip: Read Chapter 2 again to remind yourself about proteins. If you do not feel like eating much, try a Tofu Fruit Fool* which just slips down.

PANTOTHENIC ACID frees the energy in fat and carbohydrate. It occurs in so many foods, you will get enough whatever you eat.

Liver, kidney, yeast, peanuts.

BIOTIN is another vitamin which frees the energy in fat, but like pantothenic acid you can ignore it. Your body can make it, and as a rule, you do not need any extra.

Liver, kidney, yeast.

VITAMIN C (Ascorbic acid) is one vitamin most people have heard of. Cartons and bottles, especially of

Blackcurrants and their juice, other soft fruits, tomatoes, citrus fruits, green vegetables, fruit drinks, are often splashily printed with the legend 'VITAMIN C ADDED'. Most of us, therefore, realise that taking in vitamin C is a Good Thing, although fewer understand why.

In fact there are two reasons. First, vitamin C itself is vital to our health because it keeps our connective tissues healthy, helps to cure infections and heal wounds. Second, our bodies cannot make it or store it in large enough quantities so we have to take it in food regularly every day.

One problem about this is that Vitamin C is the most easily destroyed of all vitamins. It begins diminishing as soon as a fruit or vegetable is harvested and cut up, because the air on the cut surfaces destroys it. It dissolves even more quickly in water, so soaking and boiling vegetables for any length of time can be disastrous to it – especially in a copper or iron pan, or with a pinch of baking soda to keep the vegetables green. One can all too easily destroy every scrap of vitamin C which a fresh plant food contains in this way.

Some of us know from history books what happens if people are deprived of vitamin C. We have read how sailors in the days of sailing ships used to suffer from the dreaded disease called scurvy, which began with bleeding gums, and could, in the end, cause gangrene

potatoes, green peppers and other fresh and frozen fruits and vegetables – none at all in dried ones.

and death. Rampant scurvy is not a menace now, but people who do not or cannot feed themselves properly may suffer mild symptoms of it; especially elderly people who cannot handle (or perhaps afford) citrus fruits, or who only eat a few green vegetables and overcook them.

There is no need for anyone, even on a tight budget, to risk going short of vitamin C, in fact. You save on fuel, for instance, if you only cook vegetables briefly, still more if you eat them raw. Cabbage, kale, and other greens are among the cheapest vegetables worldwide. Low-cost mixed fruit drinks are often fortified with Vitamin C.

Tips: Do not waste a squeezed lemon; put it into the pan when cooking vegetables, and take out before serving.

Soft fruits and ripe stone fruits do not need cooking. Put them into boiling water or juice and leave them to soak; then serve the juice with them.

If you glance back at this list of vitamins, you will see that the same few groups of foods provide you with most of them – and that most are foods which you should eat to get the major nutrients anyway. If you are a vegetarian or eat a lot of vegetable proteins for economy's sake, make sure that you and your family eat your full quota of three to four eggs a week each (including those you put into cakes and custards). If you do eat meat, include liver once a week, and cut down on the eggs. Easy and painless ways to eat liver are in a liver sausage salad or sandwiches, or by adding cubes of liver to a steak and kidney pudding; another idea is to include some blanched, minced liver with the mince in 'burgers or a shepherd's pie.

Do not forget fatty fish in your menu planning, either. Fishburgers will appeal to kids just because they are 'finger food' but a sardine salad or pizza is usually popular too.

The other main thing to make sure of is that plenty of dark green vegetables and salad leaves feature in your family diet or (especially) if you live alone. Make sure that fruit or fruit juice features too, every day. Try a Carrot, Pepper and Orange Salad*, or add a sliced banana dipped in juice to a salad of greens and nuts, and add Wholemeal Chapons (page 60) for flavour if you like garlic.

As far as vitamin C is concerned, fruits are your friends, salads are your saviours (page 55), and careful cooking is your backstop. Remember that these mean cheaper cooking too. Salads save fuel and washing-up detergent. When you stir-fry, the quick cooking in just a scrap of oil makes up for the vitamin C loss from shredding the vegetables and saves fuel as well; see the Index for recipes. Cook all your vegetables in as little water as possible with a lid on the pan – that is quick again – and never, never throw cooking water away.

With this kind of care, even your most delicate vitamins will present no real problems. As for the others, you will find them all in foods which you will profit by choosing as sources of major nutrients; so, complicated as handling them may sound, they are really trouble-free passengers to take on board your nutrient baggage train.

MINERALS

Some of the vitamins above are included just to reassure you if you see their chemical names on package and can labels; you need not bother about them. This applies to many minerals too.

About one-twentieth of your body is made up of mineral elements (called minerals for short) which you have to get from your food. They are all substances which do essential jobs in your body, and there are two main groups of them. The ones which you need in large quantities are called the major minerals; the rest, which are just as necessary but are only needed in tiny, even minute, amounts, are called trace elements.

Here are their names.

Major Minerals	*Trace Minerals*
Calcium	Fluorine
Phosphorus	Zinc

Major Minerals	*Trace Minerals*
Potassium	Copper
Sulphur	Iodine
Sodium	Manganese
Chlorine	Chromium
Magnesium	Cobalt
Iron	Others (traces)

These minerals between them do four main kinds of work.

1) Your bones and teeth are built mainly of the major minerals *calcium* and *phosphorus* combined with help from others.
2) Every cell in your body is made partly of minerals, and those which each cell contains determine what kind of cell it is; liver cells contain different minerals from brain cells, for instance.
3) Every fluid made by your body also contains minerals; if you cry, your tears taste of salt (sodium).
4) The substances which release and carry your food energy and oxygen and set them to work also contain minerals, and cannot do their job without them; for example haemoglobin in your blood contains *iron*.

You never use up or need to replace your body's whole content of any mineral all at once, but you do lose a little of every mineral all the time in sweat and urine, and in bowel movements, so you need to top up your supplies by eating foods which contain them.

HOW MUCH OF EACH MINERAL DO WE NEED TO EAT?
You need such small quantities of the *trace minerals*, and they are present in so many different foods that most people take in enough without having to think about it; as far as meal-planning is concerned, you can ignore them.

Some of the major minerals of which you need quite large quantities are not found in all foods, however, and even when they are present your body may not be able to use them fully; for instance, if they are in a form which does not dissolve. It is unfortunately quite easy to be seriously short of calcium or iron. In the case of these minerals, therefore, you must take in *more* than you need to replace your stock; and you must see that any children in your family more than replace all their major minerals to allow extra for growing.

You may think from this that you ought to measure accurately how much of at least the three or four top major minerals you get in a usable form in your meals. But as in the case of vitamins, it is impossible, and for the same reason.

You need not worry because, in fact, you are very unlikely to take in too much of any mineral, partly because the quantities in any natural food are very small, and partly because your body generally only absorbs as much of a mineral as it needs; so your easiest and wisest course is simply to make sure that you serve yourself and anyone else whom you feed a plentiful supply of mineral-bearing foods. There are some hints on doing it cheaply without disrupting your normal meals in the following paragraphs on the more important minerals.

Calcium

You have more *calcium* in your body than any other mineral. Its main job, teamed with phosphorus (below) and with vitamin D (page 40) is to build strong bones and teeth. Almost all of it is used for this task, but about 1 per cent of it does other vital work. First, it does the essential task of making your muscles (including your heart) work properly. Second, your blood does not clot adequately unless it contains a certain amount of calcium; and calcium is constantly being swapped between your bones and blood to keep the blood content level. Your nerves also need calcium to make them function properly.

We all need to keep up the level of calcium in our bodies, but some groups of people need a good deal more than others. A new-born baby's bones are soft and bend easily; to turn them into solid bone, calcium must combine with phosphorus, and vitamin D is needed to complete the solidifying process. This teamwork is also needed to make a child's body produce extra bone as he or she grows; so a growing child needs to take in a good deal more calcium than an adult. Without it, the disease called rickets results in which the child grows up bow-legged and knock-kneed; in the early 1900s, it was so common in Britain that it was called in Europe 'the English disease', and a lurking risk of it still threatens certain groups of poorer families.

Pregnant and nursing mothers who have to supply their unborn or young babies with the means to build strong bones also need extra calcium (see page 17). So do mothers who lose a lot of calcium through frequent pregnancies. Old people also need an extra supply.

Two important reasons why rickets in children and lack of solid bone in old age are still such real risks are first that good supplies of calcium are only found in a few foods, and second that our bodies only absorb 20–30 per cent of the calcium we eat.

51

The foods themselves, although few, should not really present any problems because they are all quite cheap and easy to get. Dried skimmed milk powder is one of the best sources, but hard cheese, whole milk and milk products, white bread and flour (when they have calcium added), dried fruits and green vegetables (especially watercress) are our calcium food 'mine'. We can also get useful quantitites from: (a) the bones in sprats and whitebait, and in canned fatty fish which we usually mash and eat; (b) the 'hard' water in some places which contains calcium 'salts'; (c) oatmeal; (d) turnips. All these foods are cheap in most parts of the world where people eat a Western-style diet.

The only difficulty is that, because these foods are few and plain, they often get ignored by the people who need them most. 'Mums' prefer a cup of coffee to a glass of milk at mid-morning with their friends, and the kids prefer a bottle of pop; old people may find cutting up green vegetables and cooking them a nuisance; how many of us think of mixing dried milk into our 'burgers or of coating them with oatmeal? Thinking up gimmicks for using an ingredient you cannot even see or taste can seem a needless hassle.

It *is* worthwhile, therefore, just to check that you are getting one useful calcium-rich food every day, and that children do get milk in some form. A fruit milk shake, perhaps, or Home-Made Custard Ice Cream★.

If you are elderly, make sure that, at least, you have milky coffee or tea every day, and cheese or a sardine sandwich for supper sometimes.

Phosphorus
Phosphorus is the second most common mineral in your body, and it does many vital jobs, besides being an essential team-mate of calcium in bone-building. Every single cell in your body contains phosphorus and it plays a main part in freeing and setting to work the energy you get from food. It also regulates your body's acid balance, and some B vitamins only get to work when teamed with it. Obviously it is a very important mineral indeed.

Luckily, however, it is one you do not have to bother about at all. It occurs in most foods, and so it is almost impossible not to get enough.

Iron
More than half your body's *iron* is in the haemoglobin (page 44) which colours your blood red and carries oxygen to your various body tissues; once there, other substances containing iron make use of it to 'set alight' the energy obtained from your food.

Most of the rest of your body's iron is stored in your liver. If for any reason, you lose more iron than you get in food, and use up your stores, you will soon lack haemoglobin, and therefore oxygen; the energy from your food cannot 'burn' without oxygen, so you will feel 'as limp as a kitten'. This is an early sign of the disease called anaemia, which is most common among women and girls because they lose blood regularly in menstruation and often make no effort to boost their iron supply.

Losses due to bleeding are almost the only large-scale way the body loses iron because, although the red blood corpuscles wear out and need renewing every few months, the liver recycles the iron in their haemoglobin to make new ones. Any extra, however, has to come from food.

Meats, especially liver and kidneys, are the best source of iron because you can absorb about a quarter of all you get; liver also makes the iron in other foods easier to absorb. Vegetables, dried apricots, bread and flour, for instance, also contain iron, but you only absorb about 5 per cent of it, mostly because the rest is insoluble like calcium. If you take plenty of vitamin C (e.g. in orange juice) it improves your absorption of iron – but if you drink too many cups of tea, it reduces it!

Expectant mothers are among the women who lose iron, because they give some up to the unborn baby. The child is born with a ready-made liver store of iron to see it through the first six months while it lives on milk (which contains very little iron). However, a bottle-fed baby, especially, needs a little soft iron-rich food when about six months old, to prevent any risk of anaemia. A doctor or nurse should be asked to recommend a choice. On-the-spot professional help is always best when a baby's health or development is at stake.

An iron supplement is sometimes recommended by doctors rather than a diet change for grown-ups who show signs of anaemia. But avoid paying for drugs if you can, by making sure you do not go short of iron-rich foods.

Sodium and Chlorine (= salt)
You have *sodium chloride* (common salt, composed of sodium + chlorine) in every fluid in your body.

You lose salt from your body in sweat and urine as well as tears, and people who take violent exercise in a hot atmosphere have to take in extra salt to prevent muscular spasms and cramps. The rest of us, however, get enough salt for our normal needs in our natural foods, and get more than we need in the many processed foods to which it is added. In fact, some experts believe that we get too much, because of lot of sodium salt in one's food is thought to contribute to high blood pressure.

Babies cannot get rid of a lot of salt from their bodies all at once, so do not add salt to baby foods, even if you think they seem tasteless; they don't to your baby.

You tend to use less natural sea salt than refined table salt, and some health food enthusiasts recommend it instead of table salt which contains an additive (magnesium carbonate) to make it flow freely. Others recommend using kelp (seaweed) or exotic spices instead of sodium chloride for seasoning food. It is not too difficult, however, just to cut down on salt by serving well-flavoured meals, and it is certainly cheaper as a rule.

Potassium

Potassium, like sodium, operates in your body fluids, but, unlike sodium which functions in fluids such as blood, sweat and tears, potassium regulates the fluids inside your body cells. Like sodium, it occurs in most common foods, so you get ample for your needs in your everyday meals, especially in citrus fruits, whole grains and vegetables. Any potassium you do not need is expelled by your kidneys, as sodium is. Unless you are ill, say with acute diarrhoea, there is no risk of your losing too much.

VITAMINS AND MINERALS IN YOUR DIET

Vital as vitamins and minerals are, you should not have to alter your normal meal patterns or spend extra money to include them deliberately in your diet. If you make sensible food choices to give you the balance of protein, carbohydrate and fats you need, you will get the vitamins and minerals as a free gift in the package. Just to make doubly certain of your intake, however, here is a checklist of foods which you should make a point of including in your meals at regular intervals.

FOODS WHICH CONTAIN VITAMINS AND MINERALS
Have these at least once a week (see the Index for recipes to vary the ways in which you use them):
Canned or fatty small fish, such as sardines, sprats (if you are not a vegetarian).
Liver, liver sausage, kidneys (if you are not a vegetarian).
Eggs and hard cheese.

Yoghurt (any kind), cottage cheese.

Oatmeal.

Dried peas, beans.

Carrots.

Potatoes.

Have these at least once EVERY DAY:

One or two protein foods such as meats, fish, wholemeal (whole wheat) pasta with cheese or beans, risotto with peas.

A dark green vegetable cooked as lightly as possible.

A whole-grain cereal of some kind, and wholemeal bread.

A small helping of polyunsaturated margarine.

A SALAD (green leaves, raw or blanched vegetables, fruit etc of your choice).

A citrus fruit (orange, grapefruit, tangerine) or a tomato or the juice of one of them.

Milk (for children); milky tea or coffee or a milk product (for adults).

6. FIBRE IN YOUR FOOD

Roughage, cellulose and fibre, as we usually call it now, are all names for the same thing. It is the solid structural material of all plants, from grasses and grains to peaches; by forming the structure of the cells, it shapes the roots, leaves, veins and so on which hold their juices and nutrients.

When a cow eats grass, it gets nourishment from the fibre in the plant as well as from the nutrients in the plant cells. This is because the fibre is, in fact, a complex carbohydrate which the cow's special digestive system can break down into simple sugar. Your digestive system cannot do this, so any fibre you eat goes straight through your stomach and bowel, and out in your stools. However, nothing in the process of maintaining life is ever wasted, and fibre does other tasks in your body which are just as important as providing nourishment.

WHAT DOES FIBRE DO?

Some fruits and vegetables, and especially whole-grain cereals, contain a lot of fibre. Every seed of a grain of wheat or rice is enclosed in a coat of branny fibre, for instance. Refined white flour or white rice has had this outer layer of fibre removed in milling the grain or in polishing the rice, along with most of the nutrients in the seed. Calcium and some other nutrients are often put back into white flour for bread-making (see page 42) but the fibre is not.

When you eat refined food, especially cereal foods such as white bread or rice, or when you peel fruit or potatoes or eat 'instant mashed', your digestive system gets lazy and stops working properly, just like a lazy person. First of all, you do not have to chew these foods; 'instant mashed' or sponge cake really do 'slip down' in an instant. This means, first, that your body does not have to produce much saliva to soften them so you miss out on adding the first of your digestive juices, which is in your saliva. You do not have to give it time to get into action either and therefore you get the chance to gulp down more food without noticing it than you should ask your stomach to take all at once.

If you eat whole-grain foods, you feel comfortably fed on less food because of its bulk, and this has two effects: first, you produce more digestive juices to cope with the bulk and to chew with, and so you digest the food well; second, you tuck into fewer calories, both because you tend to eat less and because whole-grain foods contain nearly 10 per cent fewer calories than the same weight of refined starchy foods. You also absorb about 5 per cent less of the total calorie value of the food. Whole grains are clearly the slimmer's friend.

It has been known for a long time that grossly fat people are more likely to get heart disease than others; but modern thinking is that 'every little counts' and that each pound/500 g you put on over the wise top limit for your sex, weight and frame makes you slightly less likely to live to a ripe old age (see page 34). So we should look at whole-grain foods from this point of view as well as for our digestions' sake.

There is more to tell on the digestion story. Fibre slows up digestion, and this is good for your health because it slows up the rate at which sugar gets into your bloodstream, so you do not pump in at intervals a whole lot of sugar which your body does not need and therefore 'parks' as fat.

Although by slowing up your digestion of carbohydrate, fibre also slows up (and may slightly reduce) your intake of minerals, you will get enough extra vitamins and minerals to compensate for it on a meal-plan based on whole-grain foods.

You might think that fibre does enough for you by helping you to digest your food smoothly and well without piling on calories, but it does other important jobs as well when it moves on from your stomach and through your bowel.

HOW WATER HELPS

The fibre in your food absorbs a lot of water and swells up, just as rice swells when it is cooked. When you digest your food, the digestive juices break it down into its basic nutrients, fibre, and waste or excess matter it does not want. The nutrients are absorbed but the fibre and waste go straight on through your gut and out in your stools. If you drink plenty of water, the fibre is swollen and soft. The walls of your gut which alternately squeeze and relax to move the fibre and waste along can do it easily, like squeezing out toothpaste. Tight-packed fibre and waste matter without water remains in hard, dry little lumps, and is only squeezed out slowly and with difficulty. The bowel then becomes clogged, and you become constipated, and 'gassy'.

One result of constipation is that the walls of your bowel may get pitted with little pockets called *diverticulae* instead of staying smooth and elastic. Waste-containing bacteria can accumulate, and may cause serious bacteria-based illnesses after a time.

Wind, piles, varicose veins, and what we call diverticular disease, are among the common evils which a sluggish bowel can cause.

When you eat the good supply of fibre you get with whole-grain and other fibrous foods, AND drink plenty of water, the bulky, soft swollen fibre carries the unwanted waste material through you FAST. But it must have the water's help.

KEEPING YOUR TEETH CLEAN
Fibre's last contribution to your health is also important. Along with slowing up the rate at which your body absorbs carbohydrate, it slows up the rate at which bacteria grow in the plaque which you can feel on your teeth if you miss cleaning them. These bacteria in the plaque are responsible for tooth decay. Dentistry is an expensive as well as a painful way to spend any spare cash you may have, and eating whole-grain foods may help to save you from it.

All in all, fibre with your carbohydrate seems a pretty good health aid, and it is a good idea to have quite a lot of it.

WHAT KIND OF FIBRE
Although it contains plenty of fibre, you cannot eat grass like a cow. It would be a super-cheap way to eat if you could. However, we human beings do the next best thing. Although we get some useful fibre from unpeeled fruit and vegetables (and valuable nutrients with it), we get the most fibre, most easily, if we eat seeds of the grasses we call cereal plants before they are refined.

In other words, whole-grain foods: wholemeal (whole wheat) bread, flour and pasta, oatmeal, rolled oats, porridge and oatcakes, brown rice; pulses such as dried beans; wholewheat, rye and oatmeal crackers, cookies and flatbreads of various kinds!

WHAT ABOUT BRAN?
You will notice that, in one or two of the recipes in Part 2, you are told to sift the wholemeal (whole wheat) flour to lighten its texture, and then to turn the bran in the sifter back into the 'mix'. Quite a lot of people think

they can get away with eating refined white flour goods and adding a few spoonfuls of 'straight' cleaned bran (sold in most health food stores) to their breakfast cereal every day.

This is not really a good idea, although cleaned bran can be useful if you need to add 'body' to a fibreless food such as a cheese topping and you have not got spare breadcrumbs or high-fibre breakfast cereal. However, it is on the whole a pointless waste of money to buy a product with no nutritive value at all, since for the same price or less you can get a nourishing food such as oatmeal or wholemeal (whole wheat) flour.

A more important reason for using whole, natural foods, not bran, is that most of the merits of fibre only come to you with natural wholefoods. All the benefits of digesting your food more slowly depend on the carbohydrate and fibre being part and parcel of the same food, as they are in wholemeal (whole wheat) bread or pasta. The effortless ways to cut calories depend on it too, especially if you are just beginning to try high-fibre products instead of stodgy, refined ones.

HOW MUCH FIBRE?

When you begin changing over to fibrous whole-grain foods, you should start in a very small way. Use one of the ways of introducing fibre suggested below at just one of your meals on the first day or two; then increase the amount of fibre gradually over the next two or three weeks to the quantity you reckon you need. Start slowly because fibre fills up your bowel more than the refined foods you are used to, and may make you feel 'blown out' or 'windy' at first until your gut adjusts to it. (If you use plain bran, this effect is much more marked than when you use wholefoods.)

YOUR IDEAL INTAKE

No one can tell you what quantity of fibre you will need when you have got used to it. But, if you increase your intake gradually, you should find, after two or three weeks, that your bowels have adjusted to the new eating plan, and are working more smoothly, and that you look and feel better and more cheerful as a result.

Do not *overdo* your fibre, especially for children; they need less than adults, being smaller. A natural diet which includes whole-grain instead of refined cereals, plenty of fresh vegetables and fruit, should give people of any age all the fibre they need without adding any extra deliberately. But don't forget the water!

Here are some hints on how to introduce extra fibre to your own or to family meals painlessly, so that you get used to the flavour, especially of wholemeal (whole wheat) flour, almost without noticing the change.

SOME WAYS OF INTRODUCING FIBRE

1) Buy a small wholemeal (whole wheat) or high-bran loaf as part of your usual bread purchase. Use it in some of the following ways.

a) Use one white slice and one wholemeal (whole wheat) slice when making a sandwich. It looks good as well as tasting good.

b) Use a slice of wholemeal (whole wheat) toast as a 'carrier' for a supper dish such as baked beans on toast instead of your usual white bread, so that its flavour is mixed with one you know. It goes particularly well with scrambled egg.

c) Mix some wholemeal (whole wheat) breadcrumbs with your usual white crumbs when making burgers, croquettes, a crumble topping or a coating for grilled or baked fish. Gradually increase the quantity of wholemeal (whole wheat) crumbs each time you use them.

d) Cut the crusts off a slice of wholemeal (whole wheat) bread, which you will use for something else, or toast a slice lightly on both sides. Rub the crusts or both sides of the toast with the cut side of a garlic clove. Cut the crusts or toast into small cubes. Add them to a mixed salad. (They are called Chapons.)

2) Instead of changing to 100 per cent wholemeal (whole wheat) flour for your cooking, especially baking, all at once, start by mixing a little of the flour with your ordinary white flour as part of the measured quantity. Alternatively, you can get flour with some, but not all, of the bran removed. Instead of being labelled 100 per cent wholemeal (whole wheat) flour, its label shows that it consists of 81 or 85 per cent of the whole wheat. (Even if you decide to use 100 per cent wholemeal (whole wheat) flour for most of your cooking, use one of these lighter flours if you can get it for making sponge cakes, pastry, soufflés and any other dishes which hold a lot of air.)

If you are wise, you will have a practice run or two when you first use 100 per cent wholemeal (whole wheat) flour, before you offer your baked goods to anyone else. The flour may need more liquid than white flour, and until you get the 'feel' of handling it right, it can let you down by making heavy, doughy cakes or bread. This is hardly the way to persuade your family, for instance, of its merits!

3) Bought or home-made small cakes and cookies are probably the best means of introducing wholemeal (whole wheat) flour cookery into your meals. Try out two or three kinds, and get one or two established as

familiar favourites; then adventure further and try other purchases or baking, adding at the same time other forms of fibre.

4) The best way to introduce wholemeal (whole wheat) pasta is to add a few strands of long pasta or shells to a well-flavoured soup; since it keeps indefinitely, you need not worry about using only a few strands at a time, at first. You can get around to using it as a basis for a complete dish later.

5) You can introduce brown rice in the same way as pasta if you like. But its flavour is so good that you should be able to offer it as a risotto with intriguingly coloured, varied 'bits' in it right away.

6) You may already use oatmeal for coating foods for frying or grilling, especially if you keep it in stock for making porridge. Now is your chance to widen your use of this lovely nutty, nourishing food, mixed with crumbled cheese as a topping, for making parkin (it is just about foolproof!), or to mix with cracker crumbs to make a cheap 'crumb crust'* for a savoury flan – certainly cheaper than bought frozen pastry.

7) You probably already use baked beans as a supper dish, but other pulses may not be quite as familiar, and there are ways of using them which you may not have thought of. You can use sieved white beans to thicken a soup, sauce or vegetable purée, for instance, and save yourself both the trouble and fat load which making a white sauce involves. You may be wise to buy a small can if you want to use a new type in an obvious way, such as in a salad or soup. The canned products will cost less in time and fuel than if you boil a large quantity which proves unpopular; and it is not worth boiling a few.

8) As for vegetables, you need only make sure that fibre-rich vegetables feature in your meals quite often (see the list of them on pp. 62–3) and begin to add more pasta or rice and vegetable main dishes to your meals from time to time. As they become accepted as familiar, you can use them more and more often, until it becomes a habit to have a vegetable-based meal at least once a week. If you have trouble in getting the idea accepted at first, try a compromise solution by topping your vegetable dish with grilled bacon rashers or grated cheese, or add diced cooked meat or sliced sausage to the vegetable mixture as suggested in the recipe for Portuguese Vegetables* (page 148).

HOW MUCH WILL IT COST?

Besides getting some idea of how much fibre to use, you need to know how much a good-fibre diet is likely to cost.

Buying and using high-fibre foods need not be expensive. Certainly wholemeal (whole wheat) breads and flours tend to be slightly more expensive than their white counterparts because the fat and nutrients in them do not keep as long. (Breads and flours from organically grown or stone-ground cereals are a good deal more costly still, but buying these is a matter of choice.) If you can manage to make your own bread, you can save at least a third of the cost of bought bread.

Dry wholemeal (whole wheat) or spinach pasta is cheap everywhere, and certainly cheaper than fresh pasta where it is available outside its homelands. Pulses are always cheap everywhere too. Fruit and vegetable prices are not predictable. They vary enormously – with the seasons, the weather, the part of the world you live in, and a dozen other factors. When you are looking for high-fibre dishes, therefore, find vegetables and fruits with good fibre value in the list below, and choose your local 'cheapies'.

Do not turn down a bargain offer, though, because it is not on the list, or because you have not got a suitable recipe. It should not be hard to add a bit of extra fibre somewhere else in the meal, or to adapt a recipe for another kind of produce. Many vegetables and fruits, fresh and dried, are interchangeable. Most squashes for instance will 'stand in' for each other. Cucumber and courgettes (zucchini) can sometimes be swapped, and young spinach or beet leaves will do duty for lettuce, or the other way round. In a good many recipes, such as Portuguese Vegetables* (page 148), you can use canned tomatoes if they are cheaper than fresh ones; it may save you from losing a pet recipe or good meal-plan on grounds of cost.

FIBRE IN VEGETABLES (1985 figures)

Vegetables	Average portion per person	Fibre content in grams (approx)
Potatoes, peeled and boiled	100 g/3½ oz	1.0 g
baked in jackets	"	2.0 g
Beans, baked	"	7.3 g
Spinach, boiled	75 g/3 oz	4.7 g
Leeks, boiled	"	2.9 g
Carrots, old, boiled	"	2.3 g
Brussels sprouts, boiled	"	2.1 g
Cabbage,winter, boiled	"	2.1 g
Cauliflower, boiled	"	1.3 g
Onions, boiled/raw	"	1.0 g
Canned tomatoes, drained	"	0.7 g
Frozen garden peas, boiled	50 g/2 oz	6.0 g
Fresh garden peas without pods, boiled	"	2.6 g
Broccoli (tops), boiled	"	2.0 g

Vegetables	Average portion per person	Fibre content in grams (approx)
Runner beans, boiled	50 g/2 oz	1.7 g
Swede, boiled	"	1.4 g
Celery, raw	"	0.9 g
Tomato, raw	"	0.75 g
Beetroot, boiled	40 g/1½ oz	1.0 g
Lettuce, raw	10 g/⅓ oz	0.15 g
Cucumber, raw	"	0.04 g

7. HOW ABOUT A DRINK?

WATER

Strictly speaking, water does not nourish you at all, but it is more essential than any nutrient. It forms part of the basic material from which every cell in your body is made. More than half of you is water. Your blood consists largely of water, and so do most of your body's secretions. You need water for the digestion and absorption of your food, its transport through your body, for rinsing out your kidneys and the removal of waste, for regulating your body temperature, lubricating your joints and membranes, and so on. You could exist for several weeks without solid food, but only for a few days, at most, without water.

Your body's water content must be kept constant, so you need to top it up whenever it falls. You may lose as much as $2.5L/4\frac{1}{2}$ pt (or 11 + cups) a day in breathing and perspiration, urine and from your bowels, if you are active. The quantity varies, of course, but even if you do not take hard exercise, you need to put back nearly that much daily.

You get some help with this intake because you take in quite a lot of water in your solid food. On average, about 90 per cent of a turnip is water, 80 per cent of a potato and 64 per cent of a herring. Altogether, the average person eating normal meals gets about one-third of their water from their food, and a bit extra from the way the body processes certain foods. But although it is useful, it is clearly nowhere near enough to replace all the water that gets lost. Everyone has to drink, and drink plenty.

You may think you get plenty to drink in fruit juice and cups of tea or coffee in the course of the day. You would laugh at the idea that you do not drink enough; but can you be sure? For safety, most adults living in a temperate climate should try to drink four to five large glasses of fluid a day, or its equivalent in cups. In the UK, that is $1.1–1.4\,L/2–2\frac{1}{2}$ pt a day; in the USA $5–6\frac{1}{4}$ US cups. Everyone needs a bit extra after a heavy protein meal or when changing their diet to high-fibre foods (page 60). People in hot climates, and anyone who does hard physical work or sport, need a higher daily intake regularly.

JUST WATER?

Water, just by itself, is the best possible drink as well as the cheapest. A glass of water can go straight into action in your body; your kidneys and the digestive juices in your stomach and gut have to separate the 'extras' from other fluids and food before they get hold of the water needed for digestion and other processes.

Very soft water may be super for washing your clothes but it has less flavour than harder water which has useful mineral salts dissolved in it. Bottled *mineral waters* from natural springs, both sparkling and still, are usually also flavoured with mineral salts, but are a lot more expensive than tap-water; and you cannot drink the bottle which represents quite a large part of the cost. The same goes for *soda water*.

As for sweetened and flavoured *artificial mineral waters*, most of them are just bad for your teeth, your figure and your pocket (although a low-calorie tonic water and similar drinks are fairly cheap 'driver's' substitutes for alcoholic drinks).

You can choose to take most of your fluids as beverages such as fruit and vegetable juices, tea and coffee, if you want to, but include a glass of plain water at least once or twice a day as well; it gives your whole digestive system less work and cleanses it too.

MILK, CREAM AND YOGHURT

Milk is a food from whatever animal it comes. Cow's milk contains almost all the nutrients the human body needs except for being low in vitamins C and D, and in iron. However considering its rich supplies of protein, riboflavin (vitamin B$_2$) and calcium, whole cow's milk gives remarkably good nourishment value for money. Remember too that 87 per cent of it is just water! Milk is a super 'package' to take on board from that point of view as well.

Bottle-fed babies are normally fed on specially-treated cow's milk, although a few cannot cope with it; any infant milk feed should be prescribed by a doctor or nurse, and the instructions on the container must be followed precisely. The same goes for both breast-fed and bottle-fed babies when they are weaned.

Milk should still feature largely in children's diet, right through their growing period. They need it to build strong bones and teeth and for its generally rich supply of nutrients. Even teenagers putting on a growing 'spurt' need good supplies of milk in varied forms, supplemented, as for younger children, by sources of vitamins C and D, and iron. Whatever else you cut down on, do not stint the milk.

In Western-style societies, most milk is *pasteurised* – a form of heat treatment which kills off harmful bacteria. It also destroys a small quantity of B vitamins and about a quarter of the vitamin C; but you should not be depending on milk for these anyway, and will not be if you are feeding wisely. A good deal of *'long-life'* or *ultra-heat-treated milk (UHT)* and cream is also sold, which is given high heating but only for one or two seconds. It is similar nutritionally to pasteurised milk; and in spite of the packaging costs it can be a boon to people who cannot shop often. *Sterilised milk*, however, is quite violently heated with heavier nutritional loss.

In *homogenised milk*, the fat is distributed throughout the milk by a process which leaves the milk with a similar nutrient value to pasteurised milk. This is one of the developments which has made the old-fashioned pleasure of the rich 'top of the milk' – a gobbet of cream in the neck of a bottle or on top of a jugful – almost a thing of the past, at least in towns and cities. It used to be a cheap treat, and ideal if one just wanted a dab of cream to top a dessert or to mix into a sauce; it saved buying a carton. Now, as often as not, you get the milk itself in a carton.

You can get *evaporated* and *sweetened condensed milk* in cans and tubes. Long-life milk has cut out the need to keep these quite expensive forms of milk as a standard backstop. Evaporated milk has about the same nutrient value as sterilised milk, although it is fortified in some countries with useful vitamin D (page 40). Sweetened condensed milk, similarly heated, contains quite a lot of added sugar. Both have a slight caramel flavour, due to their treatment, when made up to the consistency of whole milk.

One way or another most of the whole milks drunk in Western societies, at least in cities and towns, have a nourishment value like that of pasteurised milk. But this is not true of the various forms of *semi-skimmed* and *skimmed* milk, still less of *dried skimmed milk powder*. In all of these, much of the fat has been taken off and its vitamins A and D with it, although the important protein, vitamin B_2 (riboflavin) and calcium are still intact and in some milks the A and D vitamins are put back.

Both semi-skimmed and skimmed milk are cheap and convenient low-fat sources of nutrients and can be used in many different ways if you want to keep your fat intake down and your protein and calcium intake up. Dried skimmed milk powder, in particular, can be used to make 'cream-style' sauces and added to many cooked dishes without breaking the bank. Take care, though, to replace the missing vitamins. If you cannot get the fortified milk powder, make sure that you eat enough fatty fish or liver, margarine and dark green vegetables (pages 39–40).

Low-fat yoghurt is a widely popular food with the same nutrient values as skimmed milk; some of the flavourings such as sugar which are added to vary it also add calories. *Natural* low-fat yoghurt makes an excellent and cheap substitute for soured cream in a lot of sauces and dressings, and even in cakes. *Whole milk yoghurts* when made from sheep's or goat's milk have a nutrient balance slightly different from that of whole cow's milk. All yoghurts are made by adding special, harmless bacteria to the milk which turn its milk sugar (lactose) to acid, but without destroying any other nutrients.

Cream, whether single (light) or double (heavy), pouring (table) or whipping cream, is rich in fat, and costly in both money and calories. Commercial low-fat substitutes are usually emulsified blends of butterfat, vegetable fat and skimmed milk powder. They are sometimes slightly cheaper than real cream and taste good although not quite the same.

BEVERAGES

Cocoa or drinking chocolate, along with various proprietary malted drinks, are popular (although quite costly) beverages, especially for children and old people. Cocoa itself has more food value than coffee or tea, including some iron, but the amount in an average serving is small so, as a beverage, its main merit lies in making a cupful of milk or water taste pleasant. It contains a mild stimulant, but it is one which 'jerks' the nervous system much less than coffee or tea. The various proprietary beverages have more food value (and calories) since the most popular ones contain malt extract, sugar and eggs as well as flavouring; if you do not mind that, they have the merit of being, like cocoa, tasty additions to milk when a fruit milk shake does not appeal.

COFFEE AND TEA

Coffee and tea contain no nutrients worth considering, but they both contain the stimulants tannin and caffeine. The quantity of each can vary quite a lot, depending on how the product has been processed and on how you have made a drink from it.

In the case of *coffee*, the caffeine content depends on whether you use pure ground coffee or coffee with chicory (which contains no caffeine), and on whether you use 'straight' ground coffee, *instant coffee* (which, if freeze-dried, may have a little extra caffeine) or *decaffeinated coffee* which has had the caffeine removed.

Whatever coffee you use (except decaffeinated coffee), the quantity of caffeine in it really depends on how strong you make it; and its effect on you will depend both on its strength, and on how much you drink, or have got used to drinking.

People who drink several cups of strong black coffee every day notice being deprived of it more than any ill effects. A good many people, however, find that coffee in the evening keeps them awake at night, or that coffee makes them pass water more than usual, wasting the water they have taken in with it. One effect that no one notices is that coffee, to some extent, can prevent you absorbing iron.

No coffee is cheap, but *instant coffees* may be slightly cheaper than ground coffee or coffee beans which you grind yourself in some cases. There are three types of instant coffee. Spray-dried powdered coffee is the cheapest, especially coffee with chicory; both freeze-dried coffee and spray-dried granules are more expensive. *Decaffeinated* coffee is distinctly more expensive.

Coffee bags are more expensive than instant coffee in a jar, and do not make very strong coffee. It you do not normally keep coffee in stock on grounds of cost, but want some for a special dessert or cake, you can buy individual foil or waxed paper envelopes of instant coffee, like the ones supplied to travellers in some hotels and on aircraft.

The main stimulant in *tea* is usually thought to be tannin, although in fact strong tea can contain as much caffeine as a cup of coffee. However, it is the tannin you notice. Most of the tea drunk by Westerners is fermented for a while after being harvested to give the tea leaves a stronger flavour, partly from the tannin in it. *Green teas* are unfermented, and have a flavour more like those of herb teas. Among fermented teas, China teas have the least tannin and the most subtle flavours: they are also the most costly. Indian and Ceylon teas have a stronger flavour and more tannin.

Tannin does not dissolve easily in boiling water, but it soaks out of the tea leaves if they stand, and makes the tea taste bitter. To prevent this, tea should not be allowed to stand for long after being made. A few minutes is enough to bring out the flavour from the caffeine and essential oils, and spares you the bitter taste of 'stewed' tea.

Using a *tea bag* is another way of avoiding over-strong tea because you can take it out of the pot just when it suits you, but tea bags are an expensive way to buy tea. Some only contain cheap tea leaf dust, so are poorly flavoured as well as costly. Rather rely on short standing and on using freshly boiled water for a vital flavour. Milk in the tea mollifies the taste of tannin to some extent.

Strong tea does not harm most people, but it is astringent and may slow up digestion. It can also, as can coffee, prevent you absorbing vitamin C to some extent. If you do not want to use too much tea, you could try a *herb tea* sometimes.

Herb teas are generally drunk without milk or sugar like black coffee, but it is the milk and sugar usually drunk in tea and in white coffee which give both these any real nutrient value and reviving quality. Either, however, with or without milk makes a pleasantly flavoured drink to top up your water content.

FRUIT AND VEGETABLE JUICES

Bottled and canned soft drinks such as ginger ale have little or nothing to recommend them nutritionally, but commercially made pure un-sweetened fruit juices contain good-value vitamin C, and can be used not only for drinks but for making cold sauces and salad dressings. All the various standard commercial fruit drinks must contain a minimum amount of sugar, but some contain a good deal more. The description on the container is often a fair guide to the actual quantity and to the other contents.

In a *fruit drink* so labelled in the UK, for instance, about half the contents must come from real fruit including the skins and flesh; a *fruit barley water, squash* or similar drink contains a smaller proportion of fruit juice alone, and a *fruit-ade* may contain none at all – like cola, which contains only sugar or saccharine and acid, and sometimes caffeine. A low-calorie drink must carry a full description of its contents on the container, and it is likely to be less highly coloured as well as less sugary than the standard drinks, although containing similar preservatives.

You get the best nutritional value if you can squeeze your own fruit juices and leave them unstrained. But sometimes the whole fruit may cost more than commercially-prepared juice and the cost in muscle power and processing time is certainly higher. If children demand a bought sweet drink, a 'fruit drink' with added vitamin C may be the best (although not the cheapest) choice.

Tomato juice and various *vegetable juice mixtures* are widely sold commercially, and are useful for cooking as well as for cold salad dressings and as drinks; and although they lose vitamins in cooking they can make a good alternative to sauces based on fat and flour. Remember that tomato juice has a short shelf life once opened, even in the 'fridge'; use it fast.

Refreshing and useful as they are, fruit and vegetable juices should only be thought of as a way of extending your intake of vitamins, never as a substitute for whole fruit or vegetables.

69

BEERS, WINES AND SPIRITS

Alcohol is made from fermented glucose (page 24) and it provides energy, that is calories, and very little else. Among the alcoholic drinks, only beers offer some other sugars and vitamins; the food value of all other alcoholic drinks is negligible.

Alcohol passes into your body faster than any other substance except water or glucose, because it can pass straight through the walls of your stomach and intestine into your bloodstream; so it has a very quick effect. That effect may seem stimulating, but in fact alcohol has a numbing effect on some of your nerve centres. For this reason, it deadens pain and your 'I can't cope' reaction to weariness, making worries and problems seem smaller for a while. It helps you relax temporarily, so a modest drink before a meal may help you to digest your food better if you are really tired or upset.

That is just about all alcohol can do for you; at fairly high cost too, apart from the cash you may have spent, since your worries and quite a few extra 'empty' calories will still be around to be got rid of in the morning.

8. MISCHIEF MAKERS

ADDITIVES

A good deal is said by 'natural food' enthusiasts about the evils we may suffer from chemicals and other substances which are added to our food. It is often alleged, for instance, that the contents of cans and ready-to-heat frozen meals are bulked out with cheap products which do little or nothing to nourish us, that their colours and flavours are crude and may be dangerous because they come from the laboratory not from the natural air, sun and soil, and that even the scientists who make and test them do not know what effects the chemicals may have on us sooner or later.

It is important for anyone who is menu-making on a low budget to know which of the complaints about additives are unfair, for several reasons. You cannot afford to spend money on food which gives you only low-value nourishment. Nor can you afford to pay for glamour. You cannot eat the packaging; is a fancy picture on a can really needed? Does the vivid colour of a ketchup make it cheaper to buy because it sells better? Test-market canned peas almost went off the market when their artificial colour was omitted because sales slumped. That gives food for thought.

Only you can decide whether a given product is worth its price to *you*. But, to decide wisely, you must know what you are really getting for your money.

As far as fresh unpackaged foods sold in run-of-the-mill stores and markets are concerned, you have a big advantage because you can see, if not handle, the produce which you are buying. You do not have to be a seer to know a weedy, discoloured cauliflower head when you see one. Just by looking, you can tell coarse-cut fatty mince (ground meat) from finely ground, lean, evenly pink meat, and choose whether the better quality is worth paying extra for.

Specialist service commands special prices. If you want organic foods, grown or reared without additives such as pesticides or hormones, you will soon realise that, to buy them, you will have to find one of the limited

71

number of suppliers who stock them, and pay more than in normal stores because of the small demand. But you will know what you are paying for.

The story is completely different where packaged and processed foods are concerned. The suppliers compete for an enormous mass market. The quality and flavour of each product of a given brand is consistent so that everyone who buys it knows just what he or she will get, every time. To supply the widely different tastes and needs of their thousands of purchasers, the processors compete to offer a wide variety of types, styles of preparation and flavourings. Your problem is to find out which suits you best among the unseen contents under the vivid labels. Just looking at the picture on the package is not enough.

LOOK AT THE LABEL

Legislation in some countries now demands that the majority of products, although not all, are labelled with the names of the ingredients in each pack or can, among other things. So you should be able to learn before you buy, by looking at the list of ingredients on the label, what additives the package or can in your hand holds besides your chosen main product.

Unfortunately, this is not always as simple as it sounds. All too often, the ingredients' names are not easy to understand.

First, even quite ordinary ingredients are often described by their long chemical names or just by serial numbers. They are likely to be confusingly obscure. Do you know, for instance, what Potassium L−(+)−tartrate means, or the serial number E336? In fact, they are both accurate ways of describing the common baking ingredient Cream of Tartar.

Second, even quite simple names may be obscure because they are unfamiliar or vague. *Marine shortening* is an example. *Shortening* is an American word for fat: *marine*, in this case, may mean any kind of fish oil or fat.

Terms like these are unhelpful because, if you do not understand what you read, you may suspect that your can or pack contains something you do not want or approve of. You may even think, perhaps quite unfairly, that you are being misled about its contents.

A free booklet is available in the UK, called 'Look at the Label' (see Useful Reading). Besides listing the (EEC) serial numbers and the chemical names of most of the commoner additives put into processed foods, the booklet describes the UK labelling laws briefly and clearly, telling you just what else you should be able to find out from the label.

This includes how the product must be described – for instance that strawberry-flavour*ed* yoghurt can only be so called if its flavour comes mostly from real strawberries; if the flavouring is mostly synthetic, it can only be called strawberry flavour yoghurt.

The label must also give the names of all the ingredients *in descending order of quantity* – so that, if sugar is high on the list, you can turn down that particular product and look for something less sweet. It must tell you what weight of food (plus water if it exceeds 5 per cent of the total weight) you will get in the container and what form the food is in (dried, smoked, ground or chopped, for instance), if this is not obvious to you, the shopper. Most foods, especially foods with a short 'life', must now be date-marked to show the minimum time they will stay in good condition, and the booklet describes in detail how it must be done.

All in all, you get a lot of useful information on that label.

However, you still have to interpret it, which may present problems. For instance, by law in the UK, slimming foods must be labelled with the number of calories they yield per 100 grams of the product. It is easy to assume that a carton of cottage cheese containing 113 grams or even 142 grams (which do not *look* much more than 100 grams) supplies the number of calories given on the label.

Food packagers and manufacturers are scrupulously careful as a rule not to make false claims for their products, but naturally they try to present them in the best possible light. The extra vitamin C in your fruit juice may be announced in splashy letters on the carton but the actual quantity added may be printed in very small type. As a sales boost, a fruit yoghurt may be labelled as *very low fat* instead of 'low fat'. Does it actually contain less fat than other skimmed milk yoghurts? You will probably have to read the fat content per given portion on several cartons to find out.

Then there is the matter of those chemical or vague ingredient names. There are several good reasons why they may be used, but how can you be sure it is not just to 'play down' what has been added to the can or package – and, anyway, are those additives all safe and good to use? Do they give us cheaper healthier eating than we would have otherwise, and are there any exceptions?

THE 'WHAT' AND 'WHY' OF ADDITIVES
Two main classes of 'extras' may be added to the main foodstuff when it is put into a package, can or other container for sale later.

First, there are other foodstuffs added to make the product palatable or bulky, or to save you the trouble of adding them yourself. The rice in a frozen, ready-to-heat beef curry, the sauce in a can of baked beans and the stuffing in an oven-ready turkey roast are examples. In such cases, you usually have various options. If you do not like a particular addition (such as white rice with the curry), you can, for instance, try to find the product without it, look for a suitable alternative at around the same price – or decide to put up with it.

The second, quite different class of 'extras' contains various types of additives which you cannot get away from if you buy processed foods at all. There are several types of these additives, and you will find one type or more in just about every packaged food you like to name, from bread to canned beans.

1) Most of these additives are various forms of *preservatives*. Some kill off or deactivate bacteria, yeasts, moulds and other similar living perils. Some prevent fat going rancid, or blended sauces from separating during long storage. Others stop powders such as icing sugar 'caking' in lumps, metals from causing chemical reactions in foods, and fruit from going mushy in a can.

Some preservatives are not added to the food at all. Think of how many foods you can buy in see-through vacuum packs. Those packs could not exist if hydrogen and carbon dioxide were not pumped in to replace the air which would make the food 'go off'. Another gas, nitrogen, is sprayed as a liquid on to certain vegetables to freeze-dry them with as little loss of nutrients as possible.

2) Other types of additives do still more positive jobs, helping to create stable, consistent products for you to use. Commercial margarine, mayonnaise and many other dressings and sauces would not exist if there were no *emulsifiers* to blend their vegetables and other oils with watery ingredients and *stabilizers* to keep them blended. Again, some types of jam must have acid added to make them set (just as when you make jam, at home).

3) Yet another type of additive consists of *fortifiers*, that is chemical nutrients added to foods such as bread, fruit juices or some types of dried skimmed milk.

4) The last type consists of *colourings* and *flavourings*, and the *'carriers'* which contain them.

ARE THEY ALL SAFE TO USE?

There is no short answer to this question. In all developed countries, any additives which are thought risky are banned, and all additives are tested by law as thoroughly as they can be before they are allowed to be used commercially; so are the conditions under which foods grow, are harvested or slaughtered, and are processed, packaged and sold. The processing methods are also carefully checked.

However, any substance, including many which occur in foods naturally or which your body makes itself, can do you harm if you have too much of it, or if you are allergic to it. Such substances include the synthetic additives, even though a good many are just purified forms of the same chemicals that occur naturally in your ordinary foods.

Some security lies in the fact that the permitted quantity of any chemical or other additive put into the majority of foods under British and similar regulations must be at least 100 times smaller than the smallest quantity known to do harm. However, no one can tell what the long-term effects, say over twenty years, are likely to be in the case of additives which may accumulate inside you. Some evaluation tests are too dangerous or damaging to use on human subjects, or would have to be tested on tens of thousands of people to validate them. Moral considerations inhibit other tests.

The current checks are so strict that it is unlikely that any well-established additive will prove dangerous for people who do not suffer strong allergic reactions. The effects of these additives are checked regularly in all the products already permitted to contain them, and scientists are working all the time to test their effects on other products, alone or combined with proposed new additives. Any new information – and scientists are learning new facts all the time – is applied to every foodstuff it may affect now or later. Each new discovery gives us a bit of extra security.

We get another form of security from the fact that scientists are now very much aware that they do not know what the long-term effects of certain additives may be, so they tend to be super-cautious and are constantly alert. They also *care* a great deal about food safety. In the past, this was far from being the case. Many additives were once used to 'improve' foods without any sense of responsibility. In the eighteenth century, for instance, sulphuric acid coloured with burnt sugar was used to make fake vinegar, copper sulphate gave vegetables and pickles 'an enticing green colour', so-called gin was distilled from sweetened and flavoured oils of vitriol and turpentine, and fatally poisonous sugar of lead was used to sweeten cheap, sour, or fake wine. All these were used to make cheap products for mass sale; the makers did not care what happened to their customers, even if they knew.

Modern scientists do their best to make absolutely sure that all the additives in our processed foods are non-poisonous; nutritionists are also concerned to make sure that those additives do not damage the nutrients already in our foods or prevent our bodies making use of them.

75

You may still ask, however, 'Wouldn't we be just that much safer if we did without those additives?'

DO WE REALLY NEED THEM?
Let us look briefly at the main types of additives mentioned on pages 73–4 and see.

1) Preservatives
People have been preserving food since the Stone Age. Drying, pickling, salting and smoking are all ancient ways of preventing food being spoiled by the action of bacteria, yeasts, moulds and fungi. Modern preservatives, or preserving methods such as pasteurising milk, have the same effect; they prevent food becoming unpleasant to eat or poisonous.

In the past, people preserved food simply because it was the only way they could keep alive through the winter or a drought when there were few living plants and creatures locally; there was little or no transport to bring fresh food from far away, and the journey was slow and dangerous if there was. This is still true in some parts of the world. Long ago, however, when there were fewer people, most communities managed to preserve enough food from local sources to feed themselves in times of shortage. Nowadays, there are too many people in most communities to be fed year-round in this way; and most people in cities could not process or store a bulk supply of fresh food if they got it. To feed us all, food has got to be mass-produced, preserved in vast quantities and transported long distances within our own country or from elsewhere.

In Western-style societies such as Britain, the United States and Australia, most people get a very wide variety of cheap preserved foods year-round from many different places. One can have canned tropical fruits, for instance, even in a snowy northern winter! We could all manage quite well on a more monotonous diet if we had a strong enough reason to do so. British civilian experience in World War 2 showed that. But in no way, even then, could the people do without preserved foods at all. In fact they became vital for survival. Dried fish, eggs and milk were made household staples, for instance, to give all the people cheap, nutritious food with the least use of transport.

Some very nutritious foods, such as pulses, tuna fish and pineapple are only available in processed form in most places, or are much cheaper to buy as preserved foods. Besides this, 'time is money' to many working people on a tight budget; ready-processed foods such as canned beans or freeze-dried peas save 'processing' time at home. They are also, usually,

76

less bulky than the fresh foods, so they are easier to carry home and to use. They benefit elderly people, for instance, especially those which can be kept on the shelf for easy use in bad weather.

Overall, it is probably true to say that, with these kinds of hidden savings, the less you have to spend the less you can afford to do without some preserved, processed foods, *provided* you choose ones which are nutritious as well as cheap, and do not ignore cheap, fresh raw foods.

2) Emulsifiers and Stabilizers

Can you manage without margarine? Almost everywhere, it is much cheaper than butter; and most people who prefer to eat polyunsaturated fats (page 33) probably rely a good deal on margarine made from vegetable oils along with low fat spreads. But any margarine or spread consists of processed oils which are blended with watery fluids with the help of emulsifiers, and with stabilizers which prevent it going grainy. In time, it would become distinctly unattractive to eat if these aids were not used, and it would certainly cost a lot more because it could not be stored. If you want your essential fatty acids (page 34) in a cheap, pleasant, polyunsaturated form, you will have to accept the additives which make it possible.

Most believers in polyunsaturates accept them because they do not like drinking pure oil. This is why manufacturers also use emulsion-makers to blend and stabilize mayonnaise, ice creams and most of the sauces and dressings which they include with many of their products. Without these emulsifiers and stabilizers, you might find an oily and a watery layer and sludge in your can of baked beans instead of a sauce.

3) Fortifiers

Fortified foods, sometimes called enriched foods, are, generally speaking, a good thing. They are foods to which chemical forms of natural vitamins and minerals are added by law or voluntarily, either because the nutrients have been removed in processing, *or* because certain groups of people do not get enough of them in their diet. Besides these foods, some manufacturers add nutrients to a good many more, to make their products appeal to health-conscious people.

The added nutrients are of exactly the same quality as the natural ones. The only difference is that, in some cases, you get more of them than in the original food. On the other hand, it is a matter of grave concern among a good many consumers that some foods seriously robbed of nutrients by processing do not get them all back (1986).

In the UK, for instance, all white flours (and therefore products made from them such as white bread) have had almost all the wheat germ, its vitamins and minerals, plus the bran, removed by roller milling. By law, a fair proportion of some B vitamins and iron are returned and calcium must also be added; but other nutrients found in whole-grain flours are still lacking together with the fibre (bran).

Wholemeal (whole wheat) and wheat malt flours also have calcium added. All margarines are fortified too, with vitamin A and vitamin D.

Besides these additives which the law requires, some UK and importing manufacturers voluntarily add B vitamins to breakfast cereals, and quite often add vitamin C to fruit juices. Dried and evaporated babies' (infants) milks all contain vitamin D, and the dried milks also contain vitamin A, vitamin C and iron. These are not the only fortified foods, but they are significant ones for health.

4) Colourings, flavourings and 'carriers'

Most of us are more set in our ways where our food is concerned than in any other likes and dislikes. We may enjoy the very latest in pop music or go overboard for the newest fashion colours; but we demand familiar foods and dishes and want them to have the conventional colours and flavours we know.

Colours. Processing often destroys much of a food's natural colour, whether it is done at home or commercially. The home-dried peas called carlins in Britain are greyish. Canning has the same effect as drying so, if we want canned peas, we must either accept grey-green peas or added colouring.

Although, in the past, dreadful and violent poisons were added to foods to improve their appearance without scruple (page 75), today's synthetic colourings are tested for safety with extreme care. Nonetheless, doubts remain (1986) about the effects, especially the long-term effects, of some of them.

These colourings add nothing to the flavour of foods. We do not need them. However, by making the foods more vivid, they make them more appealing, both to buy and to eat, so the majority of people demand them; and this makes the foods cheaper because they have a huge, assured market.

Until government legislation or public opinion brings about a change, health-conscious people who need to eat cheaply have either got to use time and ingenuity to prepare fresh foods, garnishings and decorations or accept a certain degree of risk.

Flavourings. Flavourings do the same job as colourings of making foods popular. They are sometimes used to heighten or improve the flavour of a processed food, either to make up for any lack in an original natural food, say in a bad year for that particular crop, or to make good any loss in processing. Sometimes, manufacturers make mixtures of natural flavours in the same way as you mix herbs and spices to put in a home-made curry.

Most natural flavourings added to foods are obtained by squeezing or distilling out the essential flavouring oils in plants. These are used to make stable, long-lasting concentrated essences which food manufacturers can use year-round to give you foods and drinks which always taste the same, even if the supply of the natural product fails or a particular crop is poor and flavourless.

Besides this, the concentrated, reliable essences are safer and cheaper to use than if the manufacturer had to process the original plants himself.

However, not all flavourings come from the plants which supplied the flavour in the first place. For instance, Western society has got used to vanilla flavouring in most sweet dishes; but not enough vanilla is grown in the world to meet the demand, so a substance called vanillin is extracted from the fibrous part of woody plants and used widely instead. Vanillin is both cheaper and purer than vanilla extract made from vanilla beans and pods, which is just as well, perhaps, as most of us are almost addicted to it.

All flavourings, natural or synthetic, are as carefully monitored as colourings. But there are many more flavourings because most of the mixtures used for even simple processed foods are very complex; a manufacturer cannot just add 'a pinch of this and that' as you can, to get the flavour you want. He must take many factors into account, such as the exact flavour of his original main ingredient to give you the same, recognizable flavour every time you buy his product.

You could do without food flavourings if you had to. Unseasoned tofu, which is tasteless, supplies the same nutrients as food which is seasoned and spiced. But if all your foods were bland, you would soon cease to be interested in what you were eating, and you would run a considerable risk of being poorly nourished. So food flavours, especially comfortingly familiar ones, have a real part to play in keeping you healthy.

Carriers. Since most flavours are made up of mixtures of substances, they have to be combined in a 'carrier' to make sure that they get distributed evenly all through a food. Various powder and liquid 'carriers' are used, all subject to the same safety tests and standards as any other additives, and necessary as a kind of packaging for them.

79

THE GRAVEST SINNERS

One more point needs making before we leave this question of whether we would be better off healthwise without most of the additives in our processed foods. Quite a number of additives are of little or no value to a health-conscious person, not because they are useless or harmful themselves but because you should avoid the foods they are used with anyway. Jam, especially smooth jam or jelly, is one such food, not because of the acid added to help some jams set, but because the jam itself is sugar-loaded. Processed cheese or cheese spread is expensive for the food value it contains compared with 'straight' cheese, regardless of the emulsifying salts used to stabilize it. Non-stick additives which prevent icing (confectioner's) sugar packing down and confectionery sticking to your pans only make the sugar easier to use, and so contribute to dietary disaster.

THE CHOICES BEFORE YOU

If you can get hold of enough varied, fresh, raw foods, and have the time, skill and energy to process them yourself competently, you as an individual could probably do without most processed foods. But it is not possible for most people to do this, especially on a limited budget. You may have to accept that you need some mass-produced foods such as margarine and canned fruits in water to live cheaply and well with some stimulus of variety in your meals, and that therefore you have to accept certain additives which help to make and keep them fit and nutritious to eat.

Often you have a choice. You can avoid some processed foods which are sugar-loaded or fatty in favour of others which are less sweet or leaner. You can choose wholemeal pasta rather than white for its extra fibre value.

You may have to take a bit of trouble to track down the best foods sometimes and to use them; for instance to buy, wash and cut up fresh salad greens instead of just buying a (usually more expensive) frozen or canned vegetable. But it can usually be done.

However, you may have to balance up priorities. If you cannot get to a store or market selling fresh produce, for instance, remember that processed foods and their additives are certainly on the whole less likely to do you harm than an incomplete or wilted choice of raw foods; remember, too, that some processed foods contribute both valuable nutrients and the variety which you need to keep your interest in healthful eating alive.

Overall, you probably need a mixture of both fresh and some processed foods to feed yourself adequately and cheaply. Whether you do it *really* well depends in both cases on what types and quality of food you chooose.

PREPARATION TIME OF RAW AND PROCESSED FOODS

You will have realised that processed foods to avoid are ones such as canned fruit in syrup in which sugar features as a major ingredient or additive. Fatty processed foods and ones which need frying before you eat them (such as frozen crumbed raw fish) are mischief-makers too. But even some 'respectable' processed products, such as frozen vegetables and dried beans, seem to have one of two big snags attached to them. They either cost more money to buy than comparable raw foods, or they cost time in preparation (and cash for fuel as well). It is hard to get round spending one or the other.

To some extent, processed vegetables, in particular, pay their way by needing no preparation time and no tools except a can-opener or knife, and by involving no waste. You do not buy any garbage except the packaging. However, this may not make up for the extra outlay in cash when you buy, even if in a town you can go for 'own brand' products in big chain-stores which are usually the cheapest. Only your budget can tell you.

Combination cooking

One way which may help is to use what I call *combination cooking*. Make your can or packet 'stretch' by adding quick-to-use ingredients ready at hand. For instance, cook frozen, canned or freeze-dried vegetables in the usual way (but a smaller quantity than usual). While cooking them, toast lightly one or two whole-grain bread slices on both sides, rub a small piece of cut garlic or onion over each side, and cut the slices into dice. Then, just before serving, mix the toast dice with the vegetables.

Alternatively, stir in a raw chopped tomato, chopped green or red pepper, or a piece of diced cucumber. Try tomato with courgettes (zucchini), green pepper with canned sweetcorn, and cucumber with frozen green beans or peas. Alternatively, add a raw, sliced onion when cooking any of them.

Try using these ideas to 'extend' canned meat or to make your eggs go further. You can make a delicious, rose-coloured omelet with one egg per person, by beating half a small chopped tomato and a teaspoonful of flour with the egg.

To get round the problem of cooking pulses, use a quick-cooking type such as lentils to make helpings for one whole cooked meal, then combine them with a small can of a long-cooking type, such as soya beans or chickpeas (garbanzos) which would be mean fare on its own. Again, add a raw, salad vegetable such as a tomato, sliced spring onion (scallion) or grated carrot at the end; the heat of the pulses will soften the raw food. You may even get helpings for two meals by just cooking one. (Serve the second one cold, as a salad.)

Another 'combo' idea using pulses is to cook raw mushrooms and a little grated onion in the same pan and at the same time as you reheat canned cooked chickpeas (garbanzos) or haricot (navy) beans. On the same principle, add a can of red kidney beans to fresh cauliflower sprigs when cooking them, combining colours and flavours, and saving fuel and washing up. There are dozens of other such 'combos' to choose from.

A tip to save vegetable preparation time is to boil red radishes, topped and tailed, as a hot 'combo' offering. They cook inside ten minutes, lose their red colour and 'bite', and look and taste like fancily-cut baby turnips. Team them with green beans, peas or carrots. (They are usually cheap to buy in season or can be grown in a window-box.) Bean sprouts are another good vegetable to add quick-to-use bulk to a meal, and offer worthwhile nourishment value, either steamed or stir-fried. For fresh vegetables, remember that the method called short-cooking (see p. 89) saves both time and fuel.

For both your health and budget, grill (broil) or bake 'burgers or fish instead of frying them. You can use much less fat or oil, or (preferably) none at all. Baking 'burgers takes longer than frying, but you may be able to cook a pudding or cake at the same time, and save fuel that way.

QUALITY RISKS

You can fix yourself a perfect diet for health on paper, and ruin it by the quality of what you buy and what you do to it. You can buy the cheapest fresh foodstuffs, and make good, attractive meals, or you can spoil most of their nourishment value by the way you handle them.

No responsible supplier in a developed country is likely to try to sell you rotten meat or fish at a bargain price, to get rid of it; but it may be temptingly easy for him to try to give you more bone or fat in your modest purchase of cheap stewing meat than the sample on the slab includes, or to fail to give you the weighed bones and head of fish after cleaning, to make fish stock. However, if you are alert you can deal with such situations. You are more likely to suffer, and will have no redress, in the case of prepacked fresh foods. You may find, for instance, when you get home from the supermarket that the stems of your celery bought in film wrapping are slimy or that the strawberries at the bottom of the punnet are mouldy.

Watch out for quality whatever you buy. Make sure that 'special offer' perishable foods in cartons have not yet reached the 'sell by' date, that foil-wrapped cheese is not seeping, that a can is not bulging or rusted and that packaged crackers feel firm and whole in their wrapping. You cannot afford to buy food – any food – just to throw it away.

Fresh foods can deteriorate in your own home faster than they do in the store. Even if you grow your own plant foods, they begin to age and lose their vitamins as soon as you harvest them. Use *any* vegetables and fruit as soon as possible after you bring them into your home. If you can only shop at intervals, say once a week, use the fresh produce first, and keep packs and cans or dried foods until the end of the period between store visits. Freshness is all-important where food produce is concerned, whether you use it raw or cooked.

Both the clock and cooking can be mischief-makers when you start to process your food. The nutrients which you have bought, or grown, are fragile; time and heat are just two of the hazards which threaten them. Whether you want to make a stew or a salad, you cannot afford to waste them; conserving their value is vitally important.

It is so important, in fact, that it is dealt with separately in the next chapter; both how to process the foods you have chosen for maximum value, and how to use them to make varied, colourful and flavourful meals which you will enjoy eating.

9. GETTING IT TOGETHER

So far, this book has been mostly about the nutrients which you ought to be eating to stay in good shape. For convenience, these nutrients have been separated into different sections. But you do not eat them like that; your 'take-away' 'burger is likely to have a flour coating and to have been cooked with oil, for instance. Your new knowledge about nutrients may be more confusing than helpful unless you know how it can be put into practice in real dishes, and how to choose and mix those dishes to make real meals which you enjoy eating. This chapter suggests a number of different ways of doing it.

Let us get one basic idea straight first. Nutrients are your servants, NOT your bosses. You do not have to pay attention to them all the time, or worry whether they have had the best possible treatment whenever you have cooked a meal or eat one prepared by someone else. You may well get concerned once you know how vital nutrients are, because you cannot tell just by looking at your meal whether it still contains all the nutrients you think it should. But worrying about whether you have boiled all the goodness out of the greens or how to make little Johnny drink his orange juice is only likely to prevent both of you enjoying your dinner; and that will not do either of you any good.

Ideally, you should try to make sure that you do take in at least some supply of every nutrient daily, particularly the B vitamins and vitamin C (pp. 46–8). But, in fact, if you are reasonably healthy, your body keeps a small stock of most other nutrients to fall back on; so, provided you make up any obvious or probable shortfall within two or three days, you should not come to any harm. It will insure you, for instance, if you fast for a day for religious or other reasons.

Instead of worrying about those over-boiled greens, therefore, just make sure that you serve green salad or slaw next day; this should cope with Johnny's vitamin C shortfall too, especially if you sneak in some grated carrot dipped in orange juice, or a chopped tomato.

GETTING AND KEEPING YOUR NUTRIENTS

Whether you are making a family meal or buying a take-away just for yourself, the most important thing in any budget catering is to choose the foods within your price range which are richest in nutrients, and to hold onto those nutrients, either by processing the foods according to proven, wise methods, or by choosing your menu with care if you eat out.

NUTRIENT HAZARDS

The nutrients you need to conserve are the proteins, including the ones in starchy foods such as pulses, and the vitamins and minerals packaged with proteins and starches, and with fats and oils. The vitamins to nurture are vitamin C and the B vitamins (thiamin, riboflavin and folic acid are the main ones); the important minerals are calcium and iron. Watch your fibre intake too.

Heat, light, air and storage time (warm or cold), soaking in water, alkalis and some metals and chemicals are the thieves and murderers which face your nutrients. Each of them prefers some victims to others. The notes on the various vitamins in Chapter 5 describe most of their misdeeds, but here is a brief 'recap'.

1) *Proteins* lose quality because some essential amino-acids become unusable with high or long *heating*, and they also become less digestible e.g. overcooked steak. The same thing sometimes happens in storage.
2) *Vitamin A (and carotene)* are destroyed by *high heat* e.g. by shallow-frying herrings in fortified margarine without a lid on the pan. Light and air also attack these nutrients in storage.
3) *The B vitamins* all get soaked out in *water*. A bit of *thiamin* also drips out in meat juices, and it is 'killed' by an *alkali* such as the pinch of baking soda in cooking water which keeps greens green. Sulphur dioxide, sometimes used in preserving, destroys thiamin too. *Riboflavin* suffers the same perils, and is attacked by *light* as well.
4) *Vitamin C is your most delicate vitamin. Water* and *air* destroy it and do so even faster if they are hot or are associated with an alkali, copper or iron. *Air* attacks, especially, the vitamin C on the cut surfaces of vegetables and fruits.

What about frozen and canned foods?
Freezing as such does not affect your nutrients to any extent. Frozen foods have almost the same nutrient content as their fresh equivalents if fast-frozen and properly wrapped; generally, frozen vegetables, for

instance, have lost no more in processing than when you blanch or cook raw vegetables straight from the ground. Plain, canned or dehydrated vegetables will also serve you nearly as well as ones you cook at home unless bicarbonate of soda or sulphur dioxide have been added to them. However, the larger the can of any food, and the more tightly-packed its contents, the more heat-sensitive vitamins will have been lost, because the can has needed longer heating to preserve the food in it.

The same goes for home cooking. It takes a longer time and more heat to cook a big piece of boiled beef right through than to grill (broil) fish fillets, so the beef loses a bigger proportion of its nutrients.

If you boil carrots with the beef for the whole of its cooking time, the chances are that they will have very little food value left indeed. Their nutrients will either have been destroyed or have seeped out into the cooking liquid. Although, in fact, most home-cooked foods seldom lose *all* their food value, they suffer serious losses of some nutrients in particular very quickly, like any other foods – notably vitamin C – if treated carelessly. You cannot afford that kind of waste.

You cannot afford to eat dud meals away from home either. The danger of some institutional meals, for instance in a college or works canteen, is that made-up meat dishes and vegetables may have been cooked in large quantities ahead of time, and then kept warm. They may then be almost valueless. *Pre-cooked* 'take-away' and fast-food meals may be depleted in the same way. If you can, choose dishes in such cases which are grilled (not fried) 'from raw' while you wait. A microwave-cooked pizza or toasted sandwich is often a good choice.

Let us look first at how you can best conserve the nutrients in the foods – any foods – which you may buy and prepare at home; it will be a general guide to the types of dishes most likely to have kept their nutrients in other eating-places too. Then we will consider how you can use the dishes you prepare or buy to make practical, interesting real meals.

CONSERVING NUTRIENTS IN COOKING
PREPARATION
Process all raw foods as little as possible when preparing them. Keep meat or fish wrapped until the last moment, then trim them into suitable pieces, cutting off unwanted material and excess fat. Cut blemishes out of vegetables and fruit, but do not peel them if you can help it; just wash and scrape them if needed. Cut them into large pieces rather than small ones. Only shred them if you have to, say if you need to get a meal ready rapidly or want to purée them. Every cut surface loses vitamins FAST.

Never, never soak vegetables or fruits in water before cooking them. Cook them as soon as you have processed them. Use as little water as possible for cooking, and 'short-cook' them as described on page 89. Remember, that hot water is a mean poacher of several vitamins, keep any cooking water left over for making gravy, a sauce or soup, or to add to a vegetable juice drink. Heat is a thief, even by itself, too. When cooked foods are ready, do not let them wait unless you have to. They will still go on losing value.

Salads

The heat hazard means that salads are your friends. In fact, a well-chosen main course salad is one of your best nutrient defences. It can guarantee you good, cheap nourishment, at home or in a packed lunch, because you can put into it almost any kind of food you like, to top up a particular nutrient.

A salad is also your chance to try out new combinations of fresh foods such as fruits, vegetables and nuts. Fruits are excellent ingredients in any modern salad, for both food value and colour. Remember that fruits such as apples and bananas must be dressed or dipped in lemon juice as soon as the flesh is exposed, to prevent them discolouring. Otherwise, only add a dressing to a salad if you really need to, and only add it at the table to prevent the saladings at the bottom of the bowl getting soggy.

Try dressing made without oil sometimes, based on fruit juice or yoghurt instead. See the index for recipes.

Using fruits or fruit juice also makes a salad an extra certain source of the most fragile vitamins. The only way you can harm them is if you cut up your salad foods too much and too soon, or soak them in water. Since you use most of them raw or just blanched briefly, you hardly use their prime enemy, heat. (This often makes a salad a bit cheaper than serving the same foods cooked.)

If possible, only prepare a salad just before a meal (except cooked grain, bean or potato salads). Wash your saladings as briefly as you can, and dry them by tossing them. Cut them up as little as possible, just like vegetables for cooking. Then serve them quickly; do not risk losing a scrap of their vitamin content and minerals by letting them stand.

Never kid yourself, either, that today's cooked vegetable leftovers will make a salad for tomorrow. You might as well eat hay.

If you live alone, remember that an open sandwich made with salad foods takes no longer to prepare than cheese on toast and often costs less; it also looks more glamorous. Indeed, salads are your picture-book foods. If you want to give a cheap party, have a salad buffet using all sorts of 'bits'. Offer open sandwiches and Ribbon Salads* spread out on platters. You will get 'Ooohs' and 'Aaahs' of surprise and pleasure.

Here are some hints to help you make really good salads without hassle.
1) Use any salad foods you can when they come into season locally. That is when they are likely to be freshest and best (although not if bought in bulk from a city market, like most supermarket supplies). Garden vegetables and fruit are best of all.
2) Choose ingredients with contrasting colours and with flavours which will remain distinct, yet will 'marry' well. See the Ribbon Salad ideas.
3) Never try to make up a salad from the last few 'tired' stragglers in your vegetable rack or fruit bowl; they will be almost valueless and will taste drab, too.
4) Do not include too many ingredients; their flavours may quarrel, and any dressing you use may not suit them all (see 7).
5) Do not soak salad foods EVER; rinse them briefly and shake dry in a sieve or colander. *Never* leave them to stand after washing.
6) Keep beetroot away from other salad foods in a mixed salad unless you 'just love' pink; serve it separately.
7) There is no need to dress a salad; most salad foods taste just as crisp and good on their own, and there is, then, no risk of their being soggy. Put oil, vinegar and seasonings on the table with a cup and a fork; anyone who wants a dressed salad can make their own dressing. Alternatively offer a light fruit juice dressing to top up vitamin C.
8) If a salad really has to wait, keep it cool with a plastic bag over it.

Mini-cooking
Some foods have to be cooked. You cannot live entirely on salads, and, anyway, you want a hot meal sometimes. Unless you live in a community of some kind, or eat all your meals out (which is usually expensive for the value you get), that means cooking at home.

The best way to hang on to your nutrients in cooking is to keep it brief. It is often said that buying cheap foods does not pay off because they generally take so long to cook. But it is not always true. Certainly stewing meat and some pulses may need several hours' cooking, so it may only be practical in a pressure-cooker or if you have cheap fuel. But chicken joints and most offal meats take no longer to cook than potatoes. Cheap fish take no longer than costly ones of the same weight and density. Some pulses and other vegetable protein foods are quite quick to cook too. For hints on making the most of them, see page 15, and pages 81–2.

Stewing. If you do have time and fuel to simmer stewing meat and you serve all its gravy with it, you get excellent protein value cheaply; the fact that much of the solid food's goodness has leached out into the liquid does not matter at all. If you make one of the stew-like fish soups called chowders, you get the best of all worlds because they are quick to cook as a rule, are non-greasy and filling. Breton Chowder* makes a splendid one-pot family meal. Cooking a whole meal in one pot like this is another bonus point for stewing.

Every country has its own traditional recipes for stews. They have been for centuries standard dishes for all peasant farming people, who in the past usually had only one fire to cook on, and one large cooking pot or cauldron. You can find excellent recipes, each with its own national flavour, in most regional and general standard cook-books.

'Short'-cooking. This cooking method is used mostly for vegetables, especially root vegetables; and it is an excellent way, perhaps the best, to conserve their nutrients (there is always *some* loss in heating, however you do it). Unless the vegetables are very young and small, they are cut into small pieces or chopped just before cooking. They are then tossed lightly with a little margarine or white vegetable fat (no more than 25 g/ 1 oz for each 600 g/1¼ lb vegetables) in a heavy, covered pan over gentle heat for several minutes. A very little boiling water is then poured over them, and they are simmered for another few minutes until just tender. They are served with their liquid. The whole process usually takes inside 15 minutes, and, in spite of the cutting up, it really does hold in the nutrients better than the usual boiling method.

'Baking' meat, fish or vegetables. If you have time and an oven, 'baking' (casseroling) in a shallow roasting pan or dish with a very little liquid, under a lid or a foil cover is another good low-fat way to conserve nutrients. Any small items of meat such as chicken joints or lambs' hearts can be cooked in this way; it is a classic method for cooking fish, squashes such as courgettes (zucchini) or pumpkin, and (in a deeper casserole) red cabbage. Cooking styles vary a good deal, but often all you need to do is to brush meat or whole vegetables lightly with oil and seasoning, dump the food in your dish with a little stock or water, cover it and leave it alone. A mixture of vegetables is usually put in with flesh foods, making a work-saving, one-dish meal. You could bake a potato dish at the same time if you want an 'extra'.

In fact, one marked advantage of oven-cooking, in spite of the relatively high cost of oven heating, is that you can save power by cooking several dishes at once, provided you choose ones which cook in about the same time, and at about the same temperature.

An easy variation on baking in a pan or casserole is to bake solid foods such as small whole fish or rolled fish fillets in lightly oiled foil 'parcels', on a baking sheet (tray). This is a pleasant way to conserve nutrients because all the aroma and flavour of the food and of any seasoning or liquid you put in the parcel is sealed in, right until you open the parcel on your plate. Foil parcels are fun for children to unwrap and may be a good way to intrigue a 'fussy eater'.

Grilling (broiling) and toasting in a dry non-stick frying-pan or skillet. These are good, speedy ways to give foods a brown, crisp surface with little or no fat. Oily fish such as mackerel need no extra fat at all. The relatively high, direct (or almost direct) heat will knock out more nutrients from thick pieces of food than milder cooking, especially if you overdo it; on the other hand, the brief minimal cooking may seal in the juices without destroying much of their value.

Stir-frying. Provided you cut up your vegetables only just before you cook, a 'stir-fry' gives you a healthful, colourful dish, and a cheap one, literally in minutes. These Oriental dishes were created by people with little or no money to spare, to use the richly coloured, varied vegetable foods of the East. Most of us can get those foods now or ones very like them, either fresh or in cans. Peppers (green, red and yellow), carrots, green and red onions, different-coloured beans, bean sprouts (best grown at home on your windowledge) and many others. If flesh foods are used, they should only form one third of the weight of the ingredients.

Briefly, the foods are cut into small thin slices or 'match-sticks' and put into groups according to how long they take to cook. One or two spoonfuls of oil are heated in a deep large frying pan or skillet (30 ml/ 2 tbsp oil will fry food for 4–6 people) and the foods are added in order, the ones taking longest to cook being put in first. They have to be stirred and turned constantly with a wooden spoon, but the whole process generally takes less than ten minutes. Seasoning, sometimes in the form of a sauce, is usually added at the end, and simmered with the 'stir-fry' for a moment or two.

Notice that, although it is called 'frying', this cooking method is really more like blanching in a thin film of oil. It uses much less oil than the fat needed for ordinary shallow frying, and any liquids you add are served with the dish. Stir-frying is also an excellent way to introduce foods such as liver which may not be popular 'in the piece'.

Mini-cooking fruit. Fresh whole fruits are the quickest, healthiest dessert of all. Those which need processing need very little. Soft fruits do not need cooking at all. Just pour boiling water over them, and leave them to steep. Blanch other fruits in the minimum amount of water for a few moments only until they are barely softened.

If fruits make a lot of juice, keep it to use as a sauce or add it to bought concentrated fruit juice. Better still, add it to home-made fruit drinks. Fresh drinks made at home are delicious, although you do need muscle power to carry the ingredients home and time to do the processing.

There are other good 'conservation' cooking methods which may suit you as well or better than the ones suggested here. These are all examples, however, of ways of cooking which cost comparatively little in work and cash for the good meals they can give you.

ENJOYING YOUR FOOD
Your meals will do you more good if they are attractive and varied as well as nourishing and cheap. It need not mean splurging on treats which you cannot afford. But there is no need, either, to martyr yourself by eating the same plain dishes day after day because they provide the cheapest reliable way to get all the essential nutrients. Varying flavours and colours, for instance, is easy even on a low budget. It may mean taking a bit of trouble, but it will be worth it when the plate in front of you holds a colourful dish with a mouth-watering aroma and a flavour you like. Enjoying your food is a real aid to digesting it fully, and thus making the most of your nutrients.

No one can tell you what to enjoy. Some people love curries and others detest them. You may be permanently addicted to apples, but it is more likely that your food preferences change with your mood, the time of day or the weather. Almost certainly, you would like to eat foods which you cannot afford, and you may look askance at the limited choice of foods you can get or can afford to buy, even if they taste good.

You need more than a pleasant-tasting product to enjoy eating it. Ideally, so gourmets say, the dish should please your eye by its colours, and tickle your nostrils with its aroma even before you taste it. You should have time to savour it without haste, and preferably good companionship, because that tends, imperceptibly, to slow up your rate of eating. Time is needed for both the appreciation and good digestion of food. If you can avoid greasy dishes to wash up, so much the better for both your health and your pleasure!

A good deal of this may seem 'pie in the sky' today as far as most of us are concerned. In particular, in lower-income groups, only retired people with little else to do probably have the leisure to spend time in eating; and, sadly, they tend to drag out their meals more as a means of evading boredom than to enjoy what is on their plates.

However, there are certain things that you, or anyone else, can do to get pleasure out of a meal.

91

First, make a picture of your dish, as far as you can. Mix colours. Always include at least one brightly coloured red or yellow vegetable in your shopping basket. At a fast-food place, ask for a salad or grilled tomato instead of French fries, not only to cut down the grease but to add gaiety. White fish, mashed potato and cauliflower in white sauce makes a sadly depressing dish. A splash of colour actually makes food seem tastier.

Don't stint scents. It may seem a nuisance if you are busy, but adding a piece of onion or scrap of leek to a savoury dish works wonders. Dried sliced onions or a sprinkling of onion powder (not onion salt) would do as a substitute. A packet of mixed dried herbs is not expensive as a rule, and is a good investment.

However pushed you are for time, stop moving (or working) while you eat. If you snatch a few scraps for your own meal while feeding the kids, try to sit down to eat them, even if you have to bob up and down. Stop reading over the letters you have typed while you eat your sandwiches at your office desk. You won't save time if you speckle them with crumbs.

Use any tricks you can think of to make your meal seem pleasant, and different from yesterday. If you eat alone, use a different plate. Turn on the radio for company, or feed the cat at the same time as yourself (but NOT off your plate). Have a little fruit juice or tomato juice before your meal, and sip it like a pre-dinner cocktail. Cut your food up carefully, and eat small mouthfuls; savour the flavour instead of bolting them down to get quit of eating. You have already taken some trouble to read about nutrients, so it is worth taking a bit more to appreciate the flavours of what you have prepared and chosen, and to savour all its merits.

MAKING REAL MEALS

It is much harder to imagine enjoying a dish of protein and vitamin C than a chicken, celery and orange salad. Nutrients, alone or combined, seem impersonal things compared with real dishes. But it would be quite impossible to list even a fraction of the real dishes composed of well-mixed nutrients which you may choose to eat; and even if one could do that, it would be futile to suggest which of those dishes are likely to be most nourishing and attractive without knowing the quality of the ingredients or how each dish has been prepared. The most that any book can do is suggest assorted nutritious foods which combine well, and so can give you all the nutrients you need in palatable dishes if properly prepared.

A technical report, such as the current British Report by the

Committee on Medical Aspects of Food Policy on the *Recommended Daily Amounts of Food Energy and Nutrients for Groups of People in the United Kingdom* (HMSO) can also, and does, suggest approximately how many calories per day the average healthy person needs at different ages, and how much of each important nutrient; similar reports or surveys are available in other developed countries. To read about these, and about how the figures are worked out, you can obtain the relevant report from government sources, as suggested in Useful Reading.

The British Report explains why some people need more than the quantity of food energy (calories) suggested for the average person, while others need less. You yourself, or members of your family, may not fit the average pattern, either concerning the total quantity of food energy you need, or the quantities of the individual nutrients. Lots of factors can vary the nutrient quantities in particular; where you live, your lifestyle, and so on. If you live in the tropics or do hard physical work you need more fluids and salt than most other people, for instance.

Since, besides this, the quantities of the various nutrients are too small to measure accurately on ordinary kitchen scales, it would be foolish here to suggest fixed quantities of nutrients or foods. You should, in any case, have children's weight checked regularly by a doctor or at a clinic, to make sure that they are getting the right amount of food to put on weight at the rate they should. As for you, once you are an adult, you need only, under normal circumstances, consult your doctor if your weight drops or fluctuates suddenly or is climbing steadily. If it stays about the same, the *total* amount of food energy you are getting, and therefore the amount of food and the size of the helpings you eat, is probably about right although you may be taking in too much of one type of nutrient and not enough of another.

Instead of giving quantities, therefore, I want to suggest, first, what sorts of foods an average healthy person will benefit from most at different ages, and then to follow that with sample menus made up of practical, pleasant dishes which should meet all your nutrient and energy needs.

GOOD FOODS TO CHOOSE

One advantage of cooking for yourself is knowing exactly how and when your dishes have been prepared. You can therefore be reasonably sure that the food combinations you use will make nourishing dishes, with their nutrients conserved as far as careful salad-making and cooking can do it. It should also be fairly easy to choose dishes in which foods help each other to give you good value; for instance a grain dish with dried peas or lentils (pages 13–14) or protein and starch mixtures (page 17), which are both good means of economy menu-making.

For your baby
A tiny baby which is breast-fed (as it should be, if possible and practical) gets a perfect menu for health. You will never have such an easy meal-planning time again! Make the most of it. Whatever you do, do not change to bottle-feeding your baby without taking professional advice. Take advice before trying your infant on solid foods, too, at around six months old.

Prepared baby foods are a good way to start (but avoid the dried varieties if possible). If the foods you pick seem tasteless to you do not worry; your baby cannot cope with extra salt or sugar until he or she is just over a year old. By then, you can pop into that little open mouth small smooth helpings of most foods you eat yourself, as well as milk. Still, however, follow the advice of your doctor, clinic or health visitor. Never risk your baby's health.

When pregnant or feeding your baby
Your menu when you are pregnant or feeding a baby must contain enough nutrients for you to make sure that your baby has strong bones and teeth, muscles and a good blood supply. Forget about slimming; you may need extra fat stores of energy, particularly if you are breast-feeding. You must also make sure that you get enough protein, and plenty of B, C and D vitamins, calcium and iron, and fibre. Take particular care to get enough milk, cheese or yoghurt, eat a green salad and an orange or some other fresh fruit every day, and have plenty of water to drink.

You can try slimming again if you need to, when your child goes to a toddlers' or play group, although running around to catch up with his (or her) activities may do the trick for you.

For your growing child
From nine to nineteen your normal, active son and daughter need a diet packed with as much of all the nutrients as your own, and perhaps more of some of them. While children are still quite small, these nutrients need to be really close-packed because the youngsters have not got room for large meals. Milk is still one of the best foods you can give them, as a drink, on cereals, in puddings or sauces. Try to make sure, too, that at

home or at school, they get enough meat, fish or cheese, and plenty of wholemeal bread, potatoes, green vegetables and fruit. If necessary, give them a packed sandwich lunch from home, including healthful snacks to prevent them contracting the nibbling habit which is expensive as well as bad for them.

As they grow older, they are likely to resent being told what to eat. Possibly the best way to encourage wise eating habits then is to persuade them, if possible, to learn about nutrition; they may be beguiled by the idea of healthy slimming or by the thought of developing energy for sport.

For you at any age
Your habits are likely to change more than your needs as you get older. *When you are young* you may be working, and enjoying various activities: sport, cycling, dancing, maybe a movie sometimes or a club party. If you work in a city, you may be tempted to rush to the office without breakfast, or want to shop in your lunch-hour. You may be living in a rented room or flat-sharing with few means of cooking. One way or another, it is easy to skip real meals and to make do with mini-snacks.

If you are studying or lonely, it is even easier; it may be all too simple to nibble too many sweets, crisps or candy bars, and do your health and your figure no good at all. (There is more about this on page 97).

Snack *meals* are all right (see page 97) if you make sure of two things: First, see that your snack meals are healthful, such as natural yoghurt and fruit, toasted sandwiches and grills with salad; keep off greasy fried foods grabbed in a hurry, doughnuts and sweetened soft drinks. Leave yourself room for the wise things instead; they do not cost any more as a rule.

Next do try, once a day, to sit down properly to eat, however busy you are, and try to choose vitamin and mineral-rich foods. Chicken liver kebabs are good if you grill or barbecue. Make a slaw sometimes, using those dark green salad leaves you may be tempted to throw away. You will only need a board and a knife. Include peanuts. You need hard cheese too, to top up calcium; you cannot dance with a broken ankle, so do not risk one.

Whole-grain bread will keep up your protein, and B vitamins and keep your bowels moving, so that you are clean all through: and, whatever else you drink, get your (unsweetened) fruit juice first. It is not too hard to say 'No' to a cola and ask for a real citrus fruit drink instead at the juice-bar. You really do need it.

If you make this sort of effort to eat sensibly, you may even find it helps you to stop nibbling and to improve your lifestyle in other ways.

If you are reading this book *in your middle years*, the chances are that you have got your meal pattern together rather better. Even if you are working, with little time to shop or cash to spare, you will understand the importance of eating a healthy diet to keep in trim, and you will have a good idea, by now, of how to do it. Here are some reminders.

Try to see that once or twice a day, you provide yourself and your family with a protein-containing meal. Use meat, fish or cheese with potatoes, pasta or bread, or settle for a dish of mixed pulses and wholegrains. (Cereals or muesli can supply protein at breakfast, to start you off well.)

Make sure that you also serve a salad of *some* kind at least once a day, and one or more lightly cooked vegetables (you will find helpful books in Useful Reading) . Supply, if you can, some fresh fruit daily. Try to use fresh, fibrous foods as often as possible, using whatever is in season because it is at peak quality then, and cheapest. If you make yourself or your family packed lunches, use wholemeal (whole-wheat) bread for sandwiches and include a fresh fruit in each pack.

If you are a vegetarian or cater for one, make sure you supply enough protein, vitamins A, D, and B_{12} as well as calcium and iron. Check the foods listed on pages 177 and 178, and stack up on them. Remember the big value of nuts.

The foods which you should try to keep out of the cupboard, both healthwise and costwise, are cream-filled cakes and sweet biscuits, packeted and canned sugary desserts, rich savoury or sweet pies and pastries. Syrup-flavoured or full-cream ice-cream and canned fruit in syrup should be banned, and so should doughnuts, fat-loaded foods or foods for deep-frying. Watch out for heavily sweetened bottles of pop and cola; if the family must have them, go for 'low-cal' types, and hopefully add fruit drinks with added vitamin C.

If you eat away from home, you should try to avoid these same foods as far as you can. Grills, not fries, salads not sweet desserts, light wines not spirits, should be your choice.

As you get older, you may drop some of your activities. You may be alone, say when your children leave home. Gradually, you are likely to slow up, and you will need slightly smaller meals although you still need all the same kinds of food. If you find it hard to get about, or if your hands do not grip too well, you may be tempted to live on sweet biscuits and tea or coffee. Make a point of drinking milk instead and try to have a fresh orange or a fruit drink with vitamin C in it at least once a day as well. As light meals, have small salads or cheese sandwiches three or four times a week. Cheese is easy to keep on your store-cupboard shelf; in a sandwich it costs less than cakes, and may save you broken bones if you slip when walking. On other days, go for chopped herring, or perhaps a kipper (kippered herring), unless the bones are troublesome. Alternatively, have soup or a cooked egg sometimes. A warm night-time drink is a good way to have a little extra milk.

REAL MEAL PATTERNS

Although suggestions are helpful, you need to translate them into a structured meal pattern and menus for making cheap, real meals at least twice a day. Some dietitians think, in fact, that we would all be fitter on four or five small meals a day provided we only eat the same amount of food in all as when we tuck into two larger meals.

A sensible meal pattern for a working or active person might therefore be a 'good' breakfast (it need not be cooked), a smallish main high-protein meal at midday, and a lighter or 'snack' meal in the evening, with a nourishing mini-snack at mid-morning and afternoon. If it is more convenient, you could swap the main meal to the evening, and keep going on a sandwich meal at midday.

If you are young with a busy schedule, or elderly with a small appetite, adapting this pattern to several small, so-called 'snack' meals may suit you quite well. Reduce the main meal to a second lighter or 'snack' one; it can be just as nutritious. Then, if you are young and active, also upgrade one of your mini-snacks to something a bit more substantial.

One thing to watch out for, though, is the difference between a true snack and a small or *snack meal*. Even if it just consists of a cheese and tomato sandwich, a so-called 'snack' should properly be counted as a light *meal* if it provides more than 200 calories. It is convenient to call it a 'snack meal' (as has been done in the earlier part of this book) to distinguish it from a conventional (usually hot) main meal, but it can be just as nourishing.

What you should NOT do if you take to a 'small meal' pattern is think that you can skip your midday or evening meal, and make up just by nibbling bits and pieces. For one thing, your stomach will never get the chance to feel it has had enough; your digestive juices will stay alert, hoping for more. For another thing, you will not remember to tot up how many calories you are getting in 'nibbles'; you may take in two or three meals' worth without noticing it – and they are likely to provide little or nothing in the way of nutrients. 'Snacks' of this kind seldom do you any good. Midnight snacks are particularly bad. All you are likely to do is load up with 'empty' calories which your body will not use up when you have gone back to sleep.

One effect of this is that you are likely to feel 'soggy' in the morning and not want your breakfast; and breakfast is important, to make you feel alert and ready for your morning tasks. Breakfast-time is a good moment to get in some of your protein for slow digestion during the day, and some of your vitamin C to make sure of it. Orange or grapefruit juice is an easy and popular way to take it (although tea or coffee may prevent you absorbing it fully, so you may prefer to have your juice at your mid-morning break!).

These ideas may be easier to follow when translated into real menus.

Breakfast

1) Orange juice.
   Muesli with raisins, moistened with milk.
   Slice of wholemeal toast, margarine and a little coarse-cut marmalade.
   Tea or coffee as you like it (milk for children).

2) $\frac{1}{2}$ apple or pear (or lightly stewed cooking apple).
   Porridge with milk and a little sugar or black treacle (molasses).
   Slice of wholemeal bread or toast, margarine or peanut butter.
   Tea or coffee as you like it (milk for children).

Mini-snacks (adults)

1) 2 or 3 small blanched carrots.
   1 rye crispbread spread with cottage cheese.
   Cup of tea or coffee as you like it.

2) 1 slice wholemeal bread spread with peanut butter, and folded.
   Glass of tomato or orange juice.

3) $\frac{1}{2}$ small carton fruit yoghurt or cottage cheese with pineapple.
   1 sweet bran biscuit (cookie).
   Glass of vegetable or fruit juice.

4) 1 small sweet apple.
   2 wholemeal or oat crackers.
   Cup of tea or coffee as you like it.

5) 1 wholemeal scone (biscuit) thinly spread with margarine.
   Orange or apple juice.

Mini-snacks (children)

1) 3 peanut butter cookies★.
   Glass of milk.

2) 1 good slice of Carrot Cake★.
   Glass of milk.

3) 1 slice of citrus cheesecake★.
   Glass of vegetable juice.

4) 2 digestive biscuits (granola cookies).
   1 banana.
   Glass of milk.

5) Wholemeal cottage cheese and banana sandwich.
   Glass of orange or blackcurrant juice with vitamin C added.

Snack or packed meals

1) Two peanut butter and tomato sandwiches made with wholemeal
   bread.
   Slice of melon or a banana.
   Tea or coffee *with milk* (milk for children).

2) Small carton of cottage cheese with savoury flavouring.
   One egg and cress and one banana and raisin sandwich made with
   wholemeal bread.
   2 or 3 young celery stalks.
   Tea or Coffee (fruit milk shake for children).

3) Mashed sardine and chopped lettuce on toast, lightly grilled if you
   wish.
   Small sweet apple, unpeeled.
   Small slice of Carrot Cake★.
   Vegetable juice health drink (fruit drink – blackcurrant or orange – for
   children).

4) Sliced hard cheese and cucumber on wholemeal toast (or as a salad
   with Chapons★).
   Canned pineapple in water with vitamin C added.

OR
Clementine (tangerine).
Raisin drop cakes.
Tea or coffee (fruit drink for children).

5) Salad-filled wholemeal pitta bread or roll (lettuce, tomato, radish or cucumber).
Cold cooked chicken wing or drumstick.
Fruit yoghurt.
Tea or Coffee *with milk* (milk for children).

Main meals

1) Breton Chowder★ (or other fish chowder).
Short-cooked Carrots and Beans★.
Spinach Salad★.
Baked apples with raisin filling.
Tea or coffee (milk for children).

2) Fishburgers★.
Grilled halved tomatoes (only grill lightly).
Green salad (lettuce, spring onion [scallion], fresh chopped parsley.
Fresh fruit (clementines [tangerines], plums, apricots or peaches if in season and cheap).
Tea or coffee (milk for children).

3) Baked Stuffed Potatoes★.
Green Bean Salad★.
Custard Ice Cream★ with fresh or canned fruit.
Tea of coffee (blackcurrant fruit drink for children).

4) Chicken Liver Kebabs★ (or mackerel).
Small baked potatoes.
OR
Boiled brown rice.
Winter (or summer) Slaw★.
Bananas and custard.
Tea or coffee (orange juice for children).

5) Risotto with Peas★.
Apple and Celery Salad★.

Custard Ice Cream★ with chopped dates or raisins.
Tea or coffee (orange juice or blackcurrant drink for children).

6) Squab Pie★.
Casseroled Potatoes★.
Carrot, Pepper and Orange Salad★.
Baked rice pudding.
Tea or coffee (blackcurrant fruit drink for children).

7) Wholemeal pasta with tomato sauce and grated cheese.
Sweetcorn and sweet pepper salad (or a three-line Ribbon Salad★).
Oatmeal Apple Crumble★.
Tea or coffee (milk for children).

8) Grilled Mackerel with Nuts★.
OR
Peanut 'Burgers★.
Lightly cooked spinach or broccoli.
Mixed salad including tomatoes, sweet pepper, cold cooked dried beans, cucumber and fruit – e.g. melon cubes, small strawberries, pipped grapes or apple cubes in orange juice.
Citrus Cheesecake★.
Tea or coffee (milk for children).

10. PROBLEM SITUATIONS

You would not be reading this book if you could buy what you liked without thinking about its cost. Shortage of cash is unfortunately a common problem, and it may seem an overriding one. But it is hardly ever the only one that people with small means have to face; commonly, it is caused by others, or is associated with them.

You, for instance, may be a senior citizen, or caring for one and having to provide special meals. You may, on the other hand, be young enough to have just left home, and are catering for yourself for the first time in a rented room with few, if any, cooking tools. You may be a single parent, or have an unemployed husband and a brood of small children, or be battling with any one of a number of other problems, or (most likely) several at once.

Any difficulties you have are uniquely your own, but most problems have common features, and in this chapter we will look at some of the commonest ones to see what can be done to trim their edges and make them a bit easier to cope with.

ALL ON YOUR OWN

There are three very common circumstances in which you may find you have to fend for yourself. First, you may be just starting out on your own; if so, your main problems, apart from money ones, may be due to lack of cooking experience and time or of knowing how to choose wisely where and how to eat out. Some hints on how you can pattern your meals have been given in the previous chapter, and you will find these and other hints drawn together below under 'Starting Off Right'.

Alternatively, you may be one of the people who are divorced or widowed between their thirties and fifties or older, and who have to adapt from housekeeping for a couple or family to cooking 'just for one', on a much reduced budget. Your inexperience is of quite a different kind.

Lastly, you may be getting on in years and facing retirement. Some of your special problems are reviewed under 'Getting On Well'.

STARTING OFF RIGHT

Obviously you have got to budget for meals as soon as you set up on your own, and equally obviously you cannot do it unless you know what they will cost. If you housekeep for yourself, this means knowing the prices of the basic foodstuffs you are likely to need, and which ones you can store or must buy fairly often.

Meal planning. Decide first what meals or snacks you will probably prepare in your own place fairly regularly, and from that, settle on a daily meal pattern which you reckon will suit you. You may be having a midday meal at work, for instance, or have breakfast provided in college or by a landlady, but need to feed yourself for the rest of the day. If you have to cater for yourself entirely, the 'small meal plan' on page 97 is an easy one to try among the various options you can choose. In making this plan, you may find it helpful to make a tentative P-C-F (protein, carbohydrate and fat) schedule, plotting when and how you expect to eat your main nutrients, and keeping an eye on your vitamins and main minerals sources too. You can use the lists of weekly and daily 'musts' on pages 54–5 as a guide.

Now list a few sample meal ideas – only a few – which ensure that between all your meals in the day, you will get all the nutrients you need. For instance, you might jot down:

Breakfast:	muesli OR mid-morning: coffee with milk, toast, peanut butter.
Lunch:	salad at Health Bar OR packed lunch: yoghurt, crispbread with low-fat spread, apple; juice drink.
Supper:	'burger OR pizza, fruit salad, coffee, at Joe's Diner.

Even if you expect to have your main meals provided or intend to 'eat out' most of the time, include some snack meals which you can make in your own home or room. You may find that you do not want to go out on a wet winter night, or that the local fast-food place is shut on Sunday. Allow for such contingencies when you do your first budgeting.

Lastly, list the dishes and ingredients you have chosen, and sally out to price them.

Prices. These prices you get at first will not stay fixed – they never do –

but you will have a cost structure from which you can start with some confidence, which will give you a good idea of how much you will have to spend to feed yourself nutritiously when you start.

Remember that, apart from canned foods, even the staple foods which you may buy to keep in stock have a limited shelf life; even dried beans toughen with age, wholemeal (whole-wheat) flour and oatmeal 'go off' somewhat sooner than refined white products (page 83). Do not buy large quantities because big packs seem cheaper until you find out how much of each product you actually use.

Varying the plan. You will almost certainly need or want to vary your meal plan and schedule from time to time. You may want to shop in your lunch-hour, or go to a concert in the evening. Adapt your plan for that day; do not let it become a burden. Include a yoghurt and an apple in your shopping if you are going to miss your midday meal, and swap your main meal to the evening if that is what you have missed. If your friends fix a barbecue, join in even if you have already had your main meal that day; skip 'bits and pieces' such as 'nibbling' snacks and sweets, but do not spoil the party by refusing to eat (see page 106).

You should not, however, make a habit of 'doubling up' – or accepting 'undesirable' foods OR drinks because it is easier than refusing. Do not kid yourself that you can make up for them by skipping meals either. Your digestion is probably fairly biddable if you are normally healthy, but it must know within reason what to expect. Whatever the reason, alternate snacking and fasting is bad for it – and you.

Meal-making at home. Anyone starting solo 'housekeeping' on a small budget is likely to have only minimal cooking equipment. You may have none at all to begin with. If this is your problem, then salads and open or ordinary sandwiches are 'for you'. You can make them with just a bread-board, kitchen knife and table knife for spreading, although a can-opener and a round-bottomed nylon sieve for salads will be a big help.

You will obviously need a spoon and fork as well as the knife for eating tools, a plate to eat off, and two or three bowls or dishes for cereals, fruit and sundries. You will also need one or two cups or mugs, and a glass for juices, milk and water. Get a jug. A bread bin, and two or three storage jars or lidded bowls are early 'musts'.

Even if you do not mean to cook at all, you must get, if you can, some means of keeping foods and drinks cool. Long-life milk 'goes off' as soon as fresh milk, once opened; and although dried milk is fine for a lot of purposes, it palls as a drink after a while. Soft and cottage cheese, yoghurt and margarine all need to be kept cool. If you open a can of sardines, and only use half of it, the rest must be kept chilled, and so must all salad vegetables until you can use them.

If you cannot beg or borrow a refrigerator, try to get an insulated box or bag which you can stand in cold water, and then keep in a cool place. In the last resort, lay hands on a plastic or tin washing-up bowl which will hold cold water; stand your storage jars or bowls in the water and cover them with wet newspaper.

After these essentials, the next thing to acquire might be a shredder or mincer (grinder) for chopping herbs and vegetables and for making sandwich fillings. A high priority, too, is an electric kettle, or plug-in saucepan which will heat water for hot drinks and packet soups.

Cooking hot meals. Even very simple cooking facilities can give you good meals; in parts of Europe, poorer people still manage well just on an open fire with a pot hung above it. However, you are more likely to find in a rented room an electric hotplate or a gas-ring. If you are starting 'from scratch', this is usually the cheapest kind of cooking appliance to add to the essentials suggested above. You will only be able to make one hot dish at a time, but that is not a big problem. You can be as warm and well-fed on one hot dish as two, and a salad is a fine accompaniment or follow-up to any hot dish.

For this kind of appliance (or for a small cooker when you acquire one) the first pieces of equiment you will need are a large and a small saucepan with lids and a frying pan, together with a large spoon for stirring, and a palette knife or slice. You can make porridge, soups and stews in the bigger saucepan, and also short-cook vegetables (page 89) and simmer fruit. If you can get a metal round-bottom sieve which fits on top of the saucepan, you can also steam vegetables over a long-cooking stew. The baby saucepan can be used for hot drinks, gravy and sauces. Use the frying-pan for omelets and stir-fries, for making toasted sandwiches (on the dry base) and for poaching fish.

Extra equipment which will be valuable when you can get it would be a second spoon (this time a wooden one), a measuring jug and scales (or measuring cups and spoons in America), a second sharp knife, and a chopping board. Salt and pepper shakers could be useful.

Salad foods. Even if you enjoy cooking, make sure you have your quota of raw foods, such as salads; look back at the list of daily 'musts' at the end of Chapter 5. Remember that salads are not only good for you, they save fuel, work and washing-up. These are extra bonuses on top of the good vitamins they give you.

The only problem which salad foods present is that they 'go off' so quickly; you do have to buy them often, and it may be difficult to buy small quantities. You cannot buy half a lettuce, for instance (although you can often get a quarter of a cabbage in city stores). In many cases, a city dweller in particular has to compromise, however. Some foods such as carrots, tomatoes, and spring onions (scallions) keep less well than others. Some, such as cooked dried beans, green peas and pineapple, can be bought in small cans. Clingfilm or food wrapping is a good investment for storing others if you are forced to. For instance, if you have to cut up a cabbage or lettuce, or cut a chunk off a cucumber, wrap the whole remainder closely, especially any cut surfaces, and put it in the coolest place you can find.

Remember that yoghurts, 'low-cal' (i.e. low-fat, low-sugar) dressings, slaw and cottage cheeses are stabilised (page 74) to keep until their 'sell by' date, provided you keep them chilled and do not open the carton. Yoghurt with cucumber and a scrap of onion makes a good back-stop salad. Chop a few radishes into it too, for their crunchiness and flavour.

'All-in'-living. Even if you get all your main meals provided, you may have to make salads (in your bedroom if needs be) if they are not included. No matter how tightly your budget is stretched, buy, beg or borrow your daily tomato and orange, if no more. Use your common sense about institutional food. Buy a wholemeal roll to eat with your main meal if only French fries are served daily, but do not refuse the mass-cooked vegetables; they will have fibre value if few vitamins. If the meals are very starchy and fatty, such as meat pies and fish fried in batter, leave some of the pastry or fat-soaked starch on your plate and add a packet of peanuts to your vegetables instead – and ask for more vegetables! Use your imagination to get round such meal problems; it is usually wiser than making an obvious fuss.

Party food. Do the same at parties. As a rule, you can quite easily refuse the 'nibbling' snacks such as fat-loaded crisps. Skip the sweet fizzy drinks too. Avoid the soggy slice of cream pie if you can (but do not upset your hostess if she made it herself). A useful thought is that there is a 'frequency factor' in nourishing yourself sensibly. One slice of chocolate cake is unlikely to harm you, but three slices one after the other, or two every evening for a week probably will. In other words, try to give yourself good eating habits, so that you choose sensible foods whenever you can without thinking about it, and then relax, and enjoy what you eat.

JUST FOR ONE
Cutting down any aspect of one's standard of living is painful. Limiting your style of eating may seem easier than most, especially if you are distressed or in turmoil after a death or divorce. Food may seem quite unimportant for a while. However, as your new lifestyle takes shape, meal problems are likely to emerge.

Shopping. First, you may well find that you do not know what to buy, to eat cheaply yet well on your own. As flesh food, for instance, your instinct may be just to substitute chops or a steak for a roasting joint, but you will soon realise how costly these are for the quantity you get, and the same goes for high-grade fish or bird meat. It is a fairly general rule that the smaller the portion the higher its price, partly because of the processing labour involved, and partly because, as a rule, small portions are taken from prime cuts or the most succulent parts of the flesh.

What is cheaper, yet good, among small-scale supplies? Small pieces of offal are one exception to the rule: a sheep's heart feeds one person well; you could casserole it while you bake a potato. Kidneys are both cheap and quick to cook; see the recipe section. A rabbit joint can be dealt with in much the same way as a heart (page 132). Stuffed vegetables are a fine standby for you, and a good way to use up leftover soft cheeses or canned fish as well. A cheap type of fish can be as tasty as a costly one if marinated in leftover yoghurt or French dressing. You might make it a challenge to find other similar ideas.

Staples raise similar problems. You may never have questioned the prices of flour, fats or milk: you just bought what was needed – and you needed more than you do now. Will you use up that bag of flour while it is still fit to use, or should you buy the smaller package, and pay a bit more for the quantity you get? You will have to house-keep carefully for a while to find out. Look out for ways to use odds and ends; for instance, make pastry with the last ounces of a bag of flour and put it in the ice-making compartment of your refrigerator.

Preparing meals. Cooking can create problems even if you have been doing it for years. You may be skilled in preparing the recipes you know, but they may not be suited to your new income and lifestyle, or to the products you must now buy.

These kinds of gaps in your knowledge may seem larger if you turn to nutritionally-focused eating at the same time, trying out foods and recipes that you may never have tried before; wholemeal (whole wheat) flour and pulses, for instance, salads and stir-fries, and cutting down on fats and sugars! Is it the best time to attempt such things? Would it be wiser to stick to the products you know until you have sorted out how to adapt *those* to your new circumstances?

This last question is the easiest to answer. There will probably never be a time when you need the benefits of wise eating more than now. You need to be in peak condition to cope with your assorted material and social problems. It may prove all too easy if you feel insecure about shopping and cooking in a new, limited style to fall back on snack eating and nibbling lots of sweet foods for comfort; focusing on a new *style* of eating will help to save you from that, and give you a sense of self-respect and independence because it is your own choice. Then, again, if you have to learn to use cheaper foods and new cooking styles anyway, you might as well turn to ones which you know make health sense.

You are also, in fact, likely to save money because, even though some foods such as wholemeal (whole wheat) flour and brown rice are a little more expensive than their white counterparts, pulses and most vegetables are cheap the world over, compared with flesh foods. Any extra costs of your 'health' foods can be set against the butter, sugar, cream, cakes and chocolate you do not buy – to say nothing of drinks! You can even make a social 'plus' feature out of your new way of eating.

As far as organising your shopping and cooking are concerned, you may find it helpful to follow the meal-planning suggestion for youngsters on pages 103–4, at least to see you through the initial phases of budget catering for yourself. Your experience and one or two cook-books from your local library will soon supplement the recipes in Part 2 to give you a full range of meals which suit your pocket *and* tastes. There are suggestions for books in Useful Reading.

GETTING ON WELL

If your income is reduced at retirement age, some of the hints on planning for budget eating in the earlier part of this section may be helpful, even if there are two of you instead of just one. But your problems in planning your meals as you get older will be different from those of a youngster or someone in early middle age, and most will still exist even when you have got used to shopping and cooking on a lower income, whether you have a partner or not.

Your meal planning. You probably still feel quite young and vigorous, since you are concerned and alert to maintain or improve your health by reading about nutrition. But everyone slows up as he or she gets older, so an older person begins to need slightly less *food energy* each day than before, although the same *nutrients* are needed even in old age. This means that although you are still living an active life, for instance taking part in community activities and gardening, you may find that you do not want quite so much to eat at each meal, especially if you are now left alone; so you may find that the 'small meal pattern' outlined on page 97 suits you quite well, although you must not slip into having sandwich-style meals all the time. You should still make sure you eat properly cooked hot meals sometimes; you will certainly need them in cold weather, and they are warming and satisfying at any time.

Your needs. One reason why you need some hot meals is that you must make extra sure you get certain nutrients, especially good supplies of iron and calcium; for one thing, you do not want to risk having brittle or soft bones in old age. You will be more inclined to give yourself enough if you vary the ways in which you eat the foods which supply them, by including both hot dishes and salads, for instance. Do make sure that you get adequate protein too, for repair work on your tissues and muscle strength, and enough fibrous foods to keep your bowels moving smoothly. Older people are prone to constipation and to diverticular disease (page 58) if they do not have enough fibre. Remember that you should avoid getting chilled, especially since you may tend to move more slowly than you used to; make sure you go for a walk every day.

Foods to choose. To meet your special needs, see that you include some oily fish such as mackerel or herring in your planning, and plenty of milk products such as cheese and yoghurt. Luckily, several kinds of oily fish are sold in small cans and are cheap as well as being good protein food, while hard cheese makes a flavourful addition to lots of easily-made hot dishes such as boiled wholemeal pasta or baked vegetables. You need only grate it over them.

It is a good idea to keep at least one of these protein foods in stock, along with a few staples such as a high-protein, high-fibre breakfast cereal, 'green' pasta and baked beans; if the weather turns nasty or you get a touch of rheumatism which keeps you indoors for a day or two, you will still be well and warmly fed.

Potatoes are another valuable standby because they keep all winter long, and can be teamed with just one egg to make a fine, easy hot meal. But there are many other alternatives, using either flesh or vegetable proteins.

Your food choice. Established habits die hard, and we all develop firm preferences for certain familiar foods, and even for particular brands. Although you accept the ideas about sound nutrition in this book in theory, you may find it more difficult than younger people to reduce your intake of some foods you like, such as sweet cakes or pastries; it is much easier to go to the cake tin or cookie jar than to make a hot meal, especially if you eat by yourself.

If this is a problem for you, skirt round it. Forget your hot meal and have light cold ones instead for a day or two. It is as easy to cut slices of bread and cheese as to cut cake. If you eat them first, and have a cup of milky tea or coffee, lightly sweetened, before you go to the cake tin, you may find you only want half the cake or even none at all. (You could sweeten your beverage with saccharin if your do not mind its aftertaste.)

Minor disabilities. Light meals which you do not have to cook can also be helpful if you have to cope with some minor disability when cooking.

Spectacles which 'mist up' in the steam from a saucepan, slightly rheumaticky finger joints which make a pan-handle hard to grip, or a painful knee which stops you getting to the stove to stop the milk boiling over can be a real nuisance, even though they do not make you disabled. Making light meals gives you 'a break' while keeping up your nutrients. (If you have real difficulties in cooking, there are many mechanical aids you can get to make housekeeping easier, and if you have a low income it is worth finding out whether a state or local authority, or a church or social group locally, can help you to get them.) It is a good idea, whether you have any minor disabilities or not, to keep a list of the staples on your shelf for making light or hot main meals. As you use them up, it will remind you of what you must buy next time you shop; and it will also remind you of foods at the back of the shelf or hidden by wrappings in the refrigerator. It is easy to become absent-minded about everyday things like food as you get older, especially if you are still active and interested in making the most of your retirement in all sorts of other ways.

CARING FOR THE FRAIL

The food needs of very old people are essentially the same as those of still-active senior citizens at retiring age, but the disabilities of age present more problems with the advancing years.

The bodily disabilities which can affect the eating habits of even a strong, healthy old person may include poor or failing sight, few teeth or ill-fitting dentures, increasing slowness in moving and inability to stretch or stoop, difficulty in handling tools such as a spoon and in gripping or lifting even a light weight. Reactions to danger slow up. The senses of taste and smell may diminish. Old bones may become increasingly brittle or soft, leading to the risk of a fracture in the event of a fall. (You should refer the more serious problems of feeding anyone who is incontinent, bedridden or senile to a doctor.)

Physical problems are not all you may have to contend with. Many old people are alert, tolerant and undemanding, but not all. Forgetfulness can become chronic, and dangerous if it leads to such things as omitting to fill an electric kettle before switching it on, or to letting it boil dry. Natural nostalgia can become an intolerant refusal to accept anything new such as a new dish or even a less popular brand of canned fruit. ('I won't like that, dear, it's not what I'm used to. . .') Demands can become querulous and constant. ('I want my dinner *now*.') It can be very difficult to distinguish between the old person's real needs and the demands which are self-assertion, a kind of defiant last stand against helplessness.

In most cities and towns and the less remote countryside of the Western world, good and caring professional advice is available to help you deal with the social and psychological problems which an old person suffers from and creates. As far as his or her day-to-day living and eating are concerned, you may have to cope on your own. Grandma's genuine needs must be met as far as possible but she must also fit in with the household's pattern. Providing separate dishes may be 'out' cost-wise, for instance, if it means buying extra foods.

A daily regime of small, snack meals and mini-snacks (pages 98–101) may well suit an old person best, although it is hardly ever a normal working family's meal pattern. One way round this is to prepare one or two light mini-snacks at the same time as the family's breakfast or packed lunches. While they must be good nourishment, the emphasis could usefully be on making them appealing to look at and easy to manage, so that the recipient can be left to eat them while household life goes on. Visual appeal is important. An aged person, like a hospital patient, may spend a lot of time brooding on the next meal; even failing eyes delight in a pretty colour pattern. Making the offering easy to eat depends on individual disabilities. Generally, crusts should be cut off bread, but a lightly toasted open sandwich cut into fingers may hold its topping better than bread. If dentures are a problem, pips must be sieved out of fruit or jam, and the valuable skins may have to be lost if you have no blender or food processor to grind them to pulp.

As far as main meals are concerned, there is no reason why an 'oldie' should not have smaller helpings of the same foods as the rest of the household, keeping in mind his or her need for easily chewed protein, fat-soluble vitamins (pp. 40–1), calcium and pulped fibre. A little milk in the helping of soup, a dab of 'marg' on the vegetables, a milk-moistened vegetable purée and a 'Granny's special' milky bedtime drink are a few of the gimmicks you might try to make sure the nutrients go down.

If a very very old person becomes so frail and disabled that he or she needs special foods and feeding arrangements and has to be fed, you should consult your doctor and perhaps try to arrange professional help, or for admission to a home.

DEALING WITH OTHERS
KITCHEN MATES
Not being a free agent can make you as tense as being left on your own. In some student flat-sharing and house group arrangements, for instance, food put in the shared refrigerator or kept in the kitchen may be

considered joint property, there for all to use. The living arrangements may be fine otherwise; but if you are trying to eat sensibly on a minute allowance, it can be frustrating or worse to find your carefully-saved orange or home-made Liverburger* has disappeared because someone felt like a midnight snack, especially if the culprit just shrugs and says, 'Well, you could have taken my fried fish instead!'

If your fellow-occupants seem unlikely to accept that your ideas matter *to you*, evasive action may be justified on essentials; for instance, you might try keeping an emergency store of non-perishables such as oranges in your own room or cupboard on the grounds that you like to 'nibble' while reading. Beyond that, compromise. If there is only white rice around, mix in some sesame seeds from your 'store', and eat it. If you can only find a piece of fried chicken, scrape off the coating, give it a quick wipe with soft paper and enjoy it. Then sometimes, if you can, bring in and make and eat a sensible meal such as a salad, and eat it right on the spot, without making an issue of it. Whatever you do, do not let yourself be self-righteous or upset; really only a medically prescribed diet is worth making a fuss about.

Sharing a kitchen with your mother-in-law may create similar problems, and demand even more tact. Whether your husband shares her views or yours, try to keep a low profile; after all, you probably want him to share your views on food if he does not already, and he may resist or turn against them if they give rise to friction.

One trick which may help is to make as many dishes as you can which look or are completely conventional. Use white bread sometimes, and top up your fibre and vitamins in some other way, or glance back at the list of vegetable protein dishes suggested on page 14, and find a good standard cookbook in the library from which you can make the unstarred ones. Then display your chosen book in the kitchen when you cook. (See Useful Reading for books to choose.)

CHILDREN

A more serious problem (also likely to be loaded emotionally) is if you feel that your children are learning to like undesirable, 'junk' foods, and turn down sensible meals as a result. This can make you frightened as well as angry, feeling that their health is at stake. They, in their turn, may resent your interfering with their chosen eating patterns, especially when they are near or in their teens. This can be still more difficult to cope with, especially if you are a working parent who has to trust them to feed themselves except for breakfast and an evening meal.

The commonest cause of the problem is that your children, like any others, want to be just like their fellows. Even small children when they first go to school see that Katie's Mummy sends her with a candy bar for 'elevenses' or that Herbie's Dad buys him a cola at the corner store when he collects him. If they visit their friends' homes, they are likely to be given sweet sticky cake and fizzy artificial drinks coloured vivid green, pink or red. How can unsalted peanuts and fresh orange juice compete with those?

The situation can be worse when they are older, especially if you cannot be at home to feed them when they return, or if they have any money to spend, say from doing chores or a paper round. That cash may well be spent on candy, so that the nutritious protein snacks you have left ready are ignored. It may mean that good food is wasted, which you cannot afford, as well as the children's teeth and general health being at risk through too much sugar.

The best way to cope with this problem as far as you can, is to make nutrition seem fun when they are young, and worthwhile when they are older. Some school-teachers are helpful in this respect. A flannelgraph 'shopping' game is easily devised and cheap to make; it can be used in the infant class or at home to show wise foods to buy and eat, and which to avoid. A classroom or bedtime 'giant-killer' story might explain that milk and cheese make one grow tall and build strong bones and that vitamin B_1 gives one energy, both for killing giants and star-quality sport. The roles of various nutrients in helping youngsters to grow big, muscled and active or slender and beautiful like their current 'crush' hero or heroine are usually quite easy to explain in fairytale or later in 'pop' terms.

Latch-key kids. As far as snack meals for 'latch-key kids' are concerned, try to choose colourful foods which have proved popular rather than novelties. Label them with fanciful names for younger children if you have time. Finger foods usually go down well because children do not have to stay indoors or find a knife and fork to eat them with. 'Burgers can be your good friends. Package them in clingfilm together with appealing (yet healthful) sweet foods such as Honey Cinnamon Squares*; at least the packets will get *opened* and absent-minded hunger may get the good protein down. If you can manage it, give a choice. The chance to 'see what looks best' is always intriguing; you might offer alternative toppings for yoghurt, for instance, such as fruit spread, chopped nuts or a *small* quantity of jam. Children who are keen on cooking (but not others) may like to make a salad for the evening meal to show off to you, and make their own mini-snacks at the same time.

Junk foods. Accept that older children will eat non-nutritious 'junk' foods away from home; rather than lay down the law about these, encourage them to choose snacks and fast-foods with real nutritional value instead. Peanuts, even if salted, are better than potato crisps which are soaked with fat as well as being heavy with salt. Fried fish is usually less greasy than fried chicken, and is certainly less soggy with saturated fats than sausages and bacon among the cheap so-called 'grills', especially if you can persuade youngsters to skip the French fries in favour of tomatoes. Popcorn has a bit of fibre in it and, even though sugared, is much less so than candies. A prepacked slice of fruit-cake is better than a doughnut at the average snack bar.

Do not push the health merits of the diet you supply yourself too hard. Your best weapon is likely to be making it appealing, both tasty and colourful. A dab of ketchup on a fishburger does very little harm. Let your child and his friend put dollops of margarine on their baked potatoes if they want to, instead of Yoghurt Dressing*, if it is made from polyunsaturated oils. At least it is not cream. (There are not many merits in being poor, but it does save you from some problems!)

When there is time, try to make your salads seem exciting but not 'odd'; children turn up their noses at food that is unfamiliar or peculiar. Offer sweetish ones sometimes. Try halved fresh pears topped with chopped nuts and raisins lightly coated with 'low-cal' salad cream, for instance. Wheedle reluctant salad-eaters to try beansprouts by growing them.

You will not win all along the line, but you may win more often than you think you are doing. Young teenagers, especially, have a habit of rejecting your ideas to your face, then producing them later to their friends (or to you) as their own. At the very least, you will have kept your own focus on nutrients alive, and have thought up a lot of new ideas for making cheap, nutritious eating more varied and interesting. That will certainly pay dividends sooner or later.

11. WHAT ABOUT ATTITUDES?

In the previous chapter, we looked at some of the problems you might face when trying to eat sensibly and healthily. Some of them were directly or largely due to lack of cash; being on your own without adequate cooking facilities, for instance. But others depended very largely on people's attitudes – on how your mates or your mother-in-law viewed the kind of food you believe you should eat to get the most out of life.

OTHER PEOPLE'S ATTITUDES
DISAPPROVAL

Other people's disapproval can cost you money, for instance in petty cover-ups such as keeping a secret store of oranges. But the cost to your nerves may be greater, for instance if you face constant teasing or jabbing remarks about 'eating rabbit food'; worse still, worrying about what your children think of you, or why they do not want to bring their friends home to eat, may begin to destroy your peace of mind. It can even make the whole idea of sensible eating based on sound nutrition seem too much to cope with.

INDIFFERENCE

Even if you do not feel under attack, other people's negative attitudes may make your eating plan more costly and inconvenient. If none of your neighbours like whole grains and similar foods, it may be difficult or impossible to find the products you want in the local shops; that may mean ranging farther afield, perhaps including a bus-ride, or carrying your goods a long way. Such a lack of demand is quite common because, on the whole, people on low incomes, especially older ones, have not had the time or leisure to get interested in new foods or in varying their food.

For this reason, your life may seem duller than it would be otherwise. If you are a 'young married', and you are thought to have 'odd' ideas about food, you may miss out on 'doorstep gossip' about meals and shopping, and you may not get asked to drop in for a chat as often as you might be. There is the problem of the kids too, and the conflict between their home and their friends' way of living.

You will have to be fairly strong-minded to face these sorts of pressures, or perhaps active disapproval, without losing your nerve. It can easily seem much simpler to throw in the towel, and say, 'healthy eating may be OK for rich folks, but it's too much of a hassle for me'.

WHAT ABOUT YOUR OWN?

If you have read so far, you are unlikely to fall 'by the wayside' now for lack of will-power. However, there is another angle to this story. You may have read as far as this doggedly just to see what you are told at the end, like reading a novel. Perhaps you feel that it has been interesting enough, but that all the stuff about nutrients at the beginning is pretty complicated and the foods do not sound very exciting; you may have to hunt for them on your day off, and you will have to learn some new recipes and drop ones you know and enjoy and which the children like too. It hardly seems worth it, when you are reasonably well as you are, bar a headache or two when you are tired after work. Why bother to change?

The first part of the answer to your question is that you cannot avoid changing. None of us can. We are all changing all the time, getting new information (like the facts in this book) and changing our habits to fit our new knowledge or physical needs. Look at Table 1 in Appendix II, and see how often your daily calorie intake must change in your life. That supplies the second part of the answer to your question. If you believe what medical scientists say, then your eating habits, like all your others, HAVE TO change periodically – that is, if you want to live to a healthy old age.

If that is so, the logical thing to do is to change them for the better; in other words to eat in the way which modern medical science shows is best for your health.

GETTING THE BEST

Getting the best where your diet is concerned need not mean (as it sometimes does in other fields) always buying the most expensive. In fact, many of the foods which are best in your diet are cheaper than less good alternatives. What you need to do is to make sure that, first, your diet includes enough varied foods to supply all your nutrients, and enough fluids and fibre. Then get into good eating habits by focusing on the nutrient-supplying foods which are best for both your health and your pocket. Here, as a final recap, are five general pointers to making wise choices.

1) Eat regularly either flesh or vegetable proteins, but include more fish and white poultry meats than red meats if you eat flesh foods.

2) For your carbohydrates, concentrate on eating a high proportion of whole-grain foods, which include the complex carbohydrate called fibre; at the same time, cut down on sugar so that you eat (and drink) comparatively little of it.

3) Concentrate, too, on eating fresh fruits and salad vegetables, to make sure of some vitamins and minerals; pick vitamin-rich foods from the list on pp. 54–5 to get others. For your vitamin D, get out of doors every day if possible. Take regular exercise, if you can; if may not *seem* to have anything to do with diet, but it can do a surprising amount to encourage good eating habits by keeping your circulation and bowels moving smoothly, and by keeping your body supple and warm as far as your age allows.

4) Eat some fats, but less than most people eat by avoiding fried foods, and obviously fatty foods; opt for the polyunsaturated fats found in most plant and fish oils.

5) Have plenty of fluids, especially WATER.

YOUR CHOICE

It does not really matter what particular foods you choose as long as you follow these guidelines. Some foods which may help you in your choice are listed in Appendix I; most are usually fairly cheap although their cost will obviously vary with where you live, the time of year and other factors. Use these lists as an extra guide to stimulate your own marketing ideas. Whatever you do, do not make yourself a martyr by trying to follow them slavishly, for instance if it is unpractical. Do not eat foods you dislike, or force yourself to eat others; rigid self-discipline is NOT the right way to give yourself good eating habits. Aim to get pleasure as well as a sense of virtue out of choosing a wise diet.

YOUR COOKING

You do not have to be a wonderful cook to eat wisely. In fact, one of the pleasures (and savings!) of healthful eating is that you should cook as little

117

as possible; salads are ideal, *and well worth getting used to on cost grounds* as well as for health. Most healthful recipes are easy; see pages 120–75 in this book, and the list of books in Useful Reading. Once you have got your supplies organised, you may well find your new cooking easier and cheaper, as well as more stimulating. Natural foods, in particular, are refreshing, and good for your figure, as well as beguiling to look at.

Eating better is not going to serve you up miracles. It needs thinking about, working to change your habits and get the process going – so that slowly but surely you will cope with life better and with less risk of illness. It means taking trouble to learn how to make the most of our fine natural foodstuffs and the enormous variety of cheap ones which modern science offer you. But surely that is worthwhile. After all, eating wisely should not be something you do as a duty, just when you want a meal. It is part of LIVING better at less cost in money and energy, and with more zest for enjoyment in everything you do.

PART 2
RECIPES

INGREDIENTS, SAUCES AND DRESSINGS

HOME-MADE MUESLI MIX
Makes 450 g/1 lb

	UK	US as UK
225 g rolled oats	8 oz	$2\frac{2}{3}$ cups
75 g brown sugar	3 oz	6 tbsp
50 g chopped almonds, hazelnuts or a mixture	2 oz	3 tbsp
50 g sultanas (golden raisins) or raisins	2 oz	3 tbsp
75 g dried apricots, chopped small	3 oz	$\frac{1}{2}$ cup (scant)
Chopped fresh fruit in season, e.g. apple, pear, banana		
Milk or yoghurt		

Place the oats, sugar and nuts on a baking sheet (tray) in an even layer. Grill (broil) for a few minutes until lightly browned. Cool, then mix in the dried fruit. Store in an airtight tin. Add chopped fresh fruit at serving time. Serve with milk or yoghurt.

WHOLEMEAL (WHOLE WHEAT) SHORTCRUST PASTRY
Makes approximately 350 g/12 oz pastry

	UK	US as UK
125 g plain flour	4 oz	1 cup
125 g wholemeal (whole wheat) flour	4 oz	1 cup
2.5 ml salt	$\frac{1}{2}$ tsp	
50 g block margarine	2 oz	$\frac{1}{4}$ cup
50 g white vegetable fat	2 oz	$\frac{1}{4}$ cup
45 ml cold water (approx)	3 tbsp	

Mix the flours and salt in a bowl, and rub in the fats to make a mixture like fine breadcrumbs. Mix to a firm but not crumbly dough with cold water. It should be pliable. Roll out on a lightly floured surface, and use as needed. Bake at 200°C/400°F/Gas 6 until set, then reduce the heat to cook any filling for a tart or pie if required.

WHOLEMEAL (WHOLE WHEAT) FLAN OR PIE PASTRY (SWEET)
Makes 400 g/14 oz pastry

	UK	US as UK
225 g wholemeal (whole wheat) flour	8 oz	2 cups
5 ml baking powder	1 tsp	
85 g vegetable fat and margarine, mixed (chilled)	3½ oz	scant ½ cup (1 tbsp)
40 g brown sugar	1½ oz	3 tbsp
30 ml cold water	2 tbsp	

Put the flour in a mixing bowl, and stir in the baking powder. Rub in the fat. Stir the sugar into the water, and add enough to the mixture to make a pliant dough, adding it in 2 or 3 portions. Wrap closely if not wanted at once, and chill.
NOTE This quantity makes one 18-cm/7-in flan case and 6 tartlets.

STABILISED YOGHURT (for cooking)
Makes 142 ml/¼ pt (½ cup + 2 tbsp)

	UK	US as UK
142 ml carton natural yoghurt	5.3 fl oz	
2.5 ml cornflour (cornstarch)	½ tsp	
Water		
Pinch of salt		

Turn the yoghurt into a saucepan and beat until liquid. Mix the cornflour (cornstarch) with a little water to make a cream, and beat it in with the salt. Bring to the boil slowly, stirring constantly with a wooden spoon. When on the boil, reduce the heat to a mere simmer, and leave uncovered for 8 minutes or until thickened. Cool and use for any dish which is heated to the boil.

FRESH TOMATO SAUCE
Makes approximately 350 ml/12 fl oz (1½ cups)

	UK	US as UK
1 kg fresh ripe tomatoes	2¼ lb	
½ clove garlic		
75 g onion (1 small onion)	3 oz	
75 g carrot (1 carrot)	3 oz	
50 g celery stalk (1 stalk)	2 oz	
Salt and black pepper (optional)		
75 ml water	3 fl oz	⅓ cup
1.5 ml honey (optional)	¼ tsp	
5 ml finely chopped parsley or basil (optional)	1 tsp	

Cut out the green stems of the tomatoes. Squeeze and break up the fruit into a large saucepan. Chop the garlic finely, and add it. Slice the onion, carrot and celery, and add to the pan, with a little seasoning if you wish. Add the water, and the honey if you use it.

Bring gently to the boil over a low heat. Cover and simmer for 1 hour or until the sauce is thick, stirring often. Taste and adjust the seasoning. Strain into a clean jug. Store in the refrigerator when cool, for 2–3 days if required. Reheat to use, and add the herb if you wish.

GINGER DRESSING
Makes 65 ml/⅛ pt (good ¼ cup)

	UK	US as UK
30 ml soy sauce	2 tbsp	
45 ml white vinegar	3 tbsp	
15 ml water	1 tbsp	
5 ml clear honey or low-sugar sweetener	1 tsp	
1.5–2.5 ml ground ginger	¼–½ tsp	

Mix all the ingredients in a bottle with a secure stopper. Shake well. Use a little, as a seasoning over green leaf salads, raw or cooked cabbage or other greens, casseroled liver or oily fish. Spread thinly on firm tofu (with a few drops of oil) before grilling it.

YOGHURT DRESSING (without oil)
Makes 175 ml/6 fl oz ($\frac{3}{4}$ cup)

	UK	US as UK
1 clove garlic		
Salt		
150 ml natural yoghurt	$\frac{1}{4}$ pt	$\frac{1}{2}$ cup + 2 tbsp
5 ml clear honey	1 tsp	
2.5 ml made mustard	$\frac{1}{2}$ tsp	
White pepper to taste		
Lemon juice to taste		

Skin and crush the garlic, and crush it with a little salt. Beat together all the ingredients, thoroughly, adjusting the amount of pepper and lemon juice to suit yourself.

APPLE JUICE DRESSING
Makes 65 ml/$\frac{1}{8}$ pt (good $\frac{1}{4}$ cup)

	UK	US as UK
30 ml apple juice	2 tbsp	
15 ml cider vinegar	1 tbsp	
Salt and pepper		
Pinch of dry mustard powder		
2.5 ml clear honey	$\frac{1}{2}$ tsp	
30 ml corn oil	2 tbsp	

Put all the ingredients in a screw-topped jar or bottle with a tight seal, and shake briskly until blended. Taste and adjust the seasoning. Shake again just before use.

MILK SALAD DRESSING
Makes 125 ml/4 fl oz ($\frac{1}{2}$ cup)

	UK	US as UK
170 g can unsweetened evaporated milk	6 oz can	
15 ml white vinegar	1 tbsp	
1.5 ml made mustard	$\frac{1}{4}$ tsp	
Good pinch of sugar		
Good pinch of salt		

Put the unopened can of milk in a saucepan, cover it with water, and simmer for 20 minutes. Cool. Open the can and put 60 ml/4 tbsp milk in a bowl. Whisk (beat) it hard for several minutes until thick and frothy. Beat in the remaining ingredients, adjusting the quantities to suit your taste. Leave to stand, chilled if possible, for several hours. It will thicken considerably if well beaten earlier. Use over a slaw, or with a rice or bean salad.

MOCK CREAM

Makes about 225 ml/8 fl oz (1 cup)

	UK	US as UK
2.5 ml gelatine	½ tsp	
120 ml water	8 tbsp	
22 ml dried skimmed milk powder	1½ tbsp	
125 ml unsalted butter or margarine	4 oz	½ cup

Soften the gelatine in half the water, then stand the container in hot water and stir until the gelatine dissolves. Cool until tepid (almost cold). Make up the skimmed milk powder with the remaining water. Melt the fat with the milk until just melted. Cool to almost cold. Turn all the ingredients into a bowl, and beat hard with an electric beater until thick. Chill for several hours or overnight before use. Beat again if a stiffer 'cream' is wanted. Use for making a fruit fool, or as a topping or filling.

If you wish, flavour the 'cream' with 2.5 ml/½ tsp spice or 15 ml/1 tbsp sweetened fruit purée before beating.

MAIN DISHES WITH MEAT OR FISH

BRETON CHOWDER
Serves 6

	UK	US
700 g any white fish (about 400 g when prepared)	1½ lb (14 oz prepared)	
900 g potatoes	2 lb	
15 ml margarine	1 tbsp	
1 onion (75 g wgt), chopped	3 oz	
20 ml flour	4 tsp	
850 ml water or fish stock	1½ pt	3¾ cups
Bay leaf, sprig of parsley and 6 peppercorns tied in a piece of cloth (optional)		
Salt and pepper		
4 slices of toast	4	
50 g parsley leaves, chopped	2 oz	2 cups leaves (⅔ cup chopped)
30 ml low fat soft cheese (optional)	2 tbsp	

Cut off the heads of whole fish; remove all fish skin and bones. (Simmer them in water to make fish stock if you like.) Cut the fish into pieces about 2.5 cm/1 in in diameter. Peel or scrape the potatoes, and cut into 2.5 cm/ 1 in cubes. Melt the fat in a large saucepan (kettle) and fry the onion in it until soft. Stir in the flour, and continue stirring for 2 minutes without letting the flour brown. Then stir in the water or fish stock, gradually at first to avoid making lumps. Add the herb bundle if used, and potatoes. Season, and simmer for 10 minutes. While simmering, cut the toast into small cubes. Keep them aside.

  Add the chopped parsley leaves to the pan, bring back to simmering point, and stir round. Then add the fish, little by little, putting in the firmest pieces first. Do not let the liquid stop bubbling slowly at the edges. Continue simmering for 5–7 minutes until the fish pieces are just cooked.

Drain the fish and potatoes in a large strainer over a basin. Remove the herb bundle. Put the fish and potatoes in a large, warmed serving dish. Keep warm under greased paper.

Reheat the fish soup until just boiling. Add the toast cubes. Serve the soup first, followed by the fish-potato dish. Top each helping of fish and potatoes with a teaspoon of soft cheese if you wish.

FILLER FISHCAKES
Serves 2 (see note)

	UK	*US* as UK
225 g white or smoked fish fillet (cod, haddock)	8 oz	
15 ml fresh chopped herbs as available	1 tbsp	
Pepper		
Salt (for white fish)		
5 ml tomato juice	1 tsp	
1 egg		
45 ml medium oatmeal	3 tbsp	
30 ml soft margarine	2 tbsp	

Poach the fish in water in a covered pan until tender. Drain, and cool. Skin, and mix in a bowl with the chopped herbs. Season with pepper, salt if used and tomato juice. Pound, mash or beat until almost smooth. Separate the egg, and beat the yolk into the fish mixture, then mix in 30 ml/2 tbsp oatmeal or oats. Shape the mixture into 2 flat round patties. Leave to stand for 30 minutes. Whisk (beat) the egg white until frothy. Sprinkle the remaining oatmeal or oats on greaseproof paper. Dip the fish patties into egg white, then coat with oatmeal or oats. Leave for 30 minutes to firm up. Use 10 ml/2 tsp margarine to grease a small ovenproof plate. Lay the patties on it, and cover with remaining margarine. Bake at 180°C/350°F/Gas 4 for about 30 minutes, until the patties are crisp and slightly browned outside. Turn once while cooking.

NOTE If left until cold, the patties firm up, and can be used for packed meals. If you just cook for yourself, eat one hot, then use the other for a snack or packed meal next day.

FISHBURGERS

Makes 6 'burgers

	UK	US
350 g cooked white fish, cooked mackerel or canned salmon, well drained	12 oz	2 cups
225 g stiff mashed potato	8 oz	1 cup
25 g margarine, softened	1 oz	2 tbsp
15 ml whole or skimmed milk, if needed	1 tbsp	
Salt and pepper		
One of the flavourings below		
Wholemeal flour or fine oatmeal for coating		
Oil for sprinkling		

FLAVOURINGS

10 ml/2 tsp lemon juice, mixed dried herbs, or tomato ketchup (catsup);
OR
30—45 ml/2—3 tbsp finely chopped mushrooms, cooked green peas or mashed sweet corn kernels.

Remove any fish skin and bones. Mash or flake the fish and mix thoroughly with the potato and margarine. Mix in the chosen flavouring, then add a little milk if needed; the mixture should hold its shape when moulded. Shape it into 6 equal-sized flattish, round cakes. Coat with the oatmeal. Lay in an oiled shallow dish, and sprinkle lightly with oil. Bake at 200°C/400°F/Gas 6 for 20–25 minutes, turning once, or until browned on both sides and well heated through. Alternatively, grill (broil) or barbecue for 5–6 minutes on each side.

GRILLED (BROILED) MACKEREL WITH NUTS AND APPLES

Single helping(s)

	UK	US as UK
1 small mackerel		
Lemon juice		
15 ml salted peanuts	1 tbsp	

2.5 ml chopped parsley	$\frac{1}{2}$ tsp
1 medium-sized apple	
A little oil	

Behead and clean the fish, but do not skin it. Rinse inside and out, and pat dry. Sprinkle inside with lemon juice. Crush the peanuts, but do not reduce them to butter; they should still be separate grains or chips. Fill them into the fish, and close the opening with a skewer or wooden toothpick.

Make 3 diagonal slashes in the skin of the fish on each side. Core the apple without peeling it, and cut across into thick rings. Brush them very lightly with a little oil. Lay the fish and apple rings in a grill pan (broiler). Grill (broil), turning once, for 5 minutes on each side. Serve with Apple and Celery Salad* or with Basic Boiled Brown Rice*.

SQUAB PIE
Serves 4

	UK	US as UK
1 kg middle or scrag neck of lamb		
(neck slices)	$2\frac{1}{4}$ lb	
1 kg cooking apples	$2\frac{1}{4}$ lb	
400 g onions	14 oz	
45 ml apple or orange juice	3 tbsp	
15 ml Worcestershire sauce	1 tbsp	
Salt and ground black pepper		
Porridge oats for sprinkling		
Boiling water		

Cut the meat into slices if needed, or ask the supplier to do it. Wipe it, and trim off excess fat. Place the slices in the bottom of a deep 2.8 L/5 pt ($6\frac{1}{4}$ pt) casserole with a lid. Core the apples, peel them and cut in round slices. Skin the onions and cut in rings. Arrange the apples in an even layer on the meat.

Mix the juice and Worcestershire sauce and sprinkle about half of it over the fruit. Season lightly with salt and pepper, and sprinkle with oats. Lay the onions on top, and repeat the sprinkling, seasoning and oats. Pour in down the side of the dish enough boiling water to cover a third of the depth of the food. Cover, and bake for $1\frac{1}{4}$ hours at 180°C/350°C/Gas 4. Leave to stand for 4–5 minutes, then skim off any fat before serving. Serve from the casserole with the liquid.

STIR-FRIED LAMB
Serves 2

	UK	US as UK
225 g leg of lamb without bone	8 oz	
15 ml oil	1 tbsp	
225 g courgettes (zucchini), thinly sliced	8 oz	
1 leek, washed and thinly sliced		
1 clove garlic, crushed		
30 ml dry sherry or half quantity soy sauce and half quantity water	2 tbsp	
Brown rice or whole-grain noodles		

Cut the lamb meat into small thin strips, discarding excess fat. Heat the oil in a deep solid frying pan or saucepan, and fry the meat over medium-high heat for 5 minutes, stirring constantly. Add the vegetables and garlic, and fry for another 3 minutes still stirring. Add the sherry or soy mixture and simmer for 2 minutes. Serve at once over brown rice or wholewheat noodles.

LIVER KEBABS
Serves 2

	UK	US as UK
125 g lamb's liver	4 oz	
50 g piece large onion ($\frac{1}{4}$ onion)	2 oz	
$\frac{1}{2}$ large red pepper, seeded		
Salt and pepper		
125–175 g wholewheat pasta shells or noodles	4–6 oz	
Oil		
Margarine (optional)		

Cut the liver into 12 square-shaped pieces. Cut the onion and pepper into similar pieces. Bring a large pan of slightly salted water to the boil, tip in the pasta and bring back to the boil. Reduce the heat to give moderate bubbling, and cook until tender. While cooking, thread the pieces of liver, onion and pepper on 2 long skewers, beginning with liver and ending with pepper. Season the kebabs and brush lightly with oil. Grill (broil) until cooked through, using moderate heat and turning frequently (about 10 minutes). Drain the pasta when done, and tip into a shallow dish in an even layer. Lay the kebabs on top to serve.

If you wish, dot the pasta with margarine before serving.

ROYAL KIDNEY DISH
Single helping(s)

	UK	US
150–175 g ox (beef) kidney	5–6 oz	
15 ml 85% extraction flour	1 tbsp	
Salt and pepper		
15 ml margarine	1 tbsp	
25 g button mushrooms, chopped	1 oz	
5 ml chopped parsley	1 tsp	
1 spring onion (scallion) chopped (green and white parts)		
5 ml Worcestershire sauce	1 tsp	
5 ml lemon juice	1 tsp	
65 ml beef stock or thin gravy	$\frac{1}{8}$ pt	$\frac{1}{4}$ cup + 1 tbsp
Triangles of toasted wholemeal bread		

Core the kidney, and cut it across into thin small slices. Season the flour with salt and pepper, and dust the slices with a little of it. Sear them briefly in the fat over moderate heat, turning them with a spatula. Add the mushrooms, parsley and onion, reduce the heat and turn them in the fat until well coated; then sprinkle in the remaining flour and stir round. Remove from the heat, and add the Worcestershire sauce, lemon juice and stock or gravy. Simmer for 3–4 minutes, until the onion is soft and the sauce reduced almost to a glaze. Add a little more stock or water if it looks like drying out. Spoon onto a warmed plate, and arrange toast triangles round the dish.

CHICKEN LIVER STIR-FRY
Serves 4

	UK	US
125 g bacon rashers (slices without rind)	4 oz	
$\frac{1}{2}$ medium onion, chopped		

50 g green pepper, chopped	2 oz	
350 g chicken livers, halved	12 oz	
45 ml seasoned flour	3 tbsp	
15 ml oil	1 tbsp	
225 ml water	8 fl oz	1 cup
3 soaked, stoned prunes, chopped		
450 g boiled brown rice (hot)	1 lb	

Chop the bacon and mix with the onion and pepper. Coat the chicken livers with the flour. Heat the oil in a frying pan, and put in the bacon, onion and pepper mixture. Stir with a wooden spoon until the onion softens. Add the livers, and continue stirring until they are browned outside but still pink inside. Add the water slowly, and stir until the liquid thickens. Add the chopped prunes and simmer for 1 minute. Dish up on the drained, hot or reheated rice.

LIVERBURGERS

Makes 6 'burgers

	UK	US as UK
450 g beef mince (ground beef)	1 lb	
125 g ox (beef) liver finely chopped or minced (ground)	4 oz	
30 ml grated onion	2 tbsp	
Freshly ground black pepper		
5 ml Worcestershire sauce	1 tsp	
Oil for grilling		
Tabasco sauce and lemon juice for sprinkling		
Chopped parsley		

Mix together the beef, liver and onion, and season with pepper and Worcestershire sauce. Shape into 6 flat round patties. Brush with oil and grill (broil) using medium heat for about 5 minutes. Turn over and cook to the degree you prefer, from 2–4 minutes, turning the heat down after half a minute. Serve sprinkled with Tabasco, lemon juice and chopped parsley.

BAKED SPICY CHICKEN OR RABBIT
Single helping(s)

	UK	US as UK
1 chicken or rabbit leg joint		
1 small leek, green and white parts		
$\frac{1}{2}$ sweet red pepper		
60 ml Ginger Dressing*	4 tbsp	
90 ml water	6 tbsp	
10 ml margarine (optional)	2 tsp	

Wash and dry the joint. Slice the leek into 5 mm/$\frac{1}{4}$ in rounds. De-seed the pepper if needed and cut into small strips. Jumble the vegetables in a shallow heatproof bowl, and lay the joint on top. Mix together the ginger dressing and water and pour it over the joint. Cover tightly with foil, and bake at 180°C/350°F/Gas 4 for about 30 minutes. Prod with a skewer to test for tenderness. No blood should come out when it is inserted in the thickest part of the meat.

MRS VICKERY'S GINGERED RABBIT
Serves 4

	UK	US
1 rabbit, about 1.1 kg/2$\frac{1}{2}$ lb or 900 g/2 lb after preparation		
30 ml margarine	2 tbsp	
15 ml oil	1 tbsp	
15 ml seasoned flour	1 tbsp	
10 ml curry powder	2 tsp	
1 small onion, finely chopped		
350 ml white or chicken stock	12 fl oz	1$\frac{1}{2}$ cups
75 g dried apricots, finely chopped (see note)	3 oz	
25 g flaked almonds	1 oz	
2 pieces of preserved stem ginger		
30 ml syrup from ginger jar	2 tbsp	
Salt and pepper		
Lemon wedges (optional)		

Skin and paunch a wild rabbit as soon as it is shot. Hang it for 24 hours. Behead it, discard the forelegs, and cut the rest into 4 joints (shoulders and ribs, saddle and two hind legs). Joint a tame or ready-skinned rabbit in the same way.

Wash and dry the rabbit joints. Put the fat and oil in a deep flameproof casserole or saucepan. Dust the joints with some of the seasoned flour, and turn in the fat until browned. Remove and drain on soft paper. Add the onion to the remaining fat and fry until browned. Add the remaining flour and the curry powder and stir in. Continue frying and stirring for 3 minutes. Stir in half the stock, and bring to the boil. Add the dried fruit and almonds. Lay the rabbit joints on top, and sprinkle with the chopped ginger and syrup. Season. Cover and simmer for $1-1\frac{1}{2}$ hrs (1 hr for tame rabbit) adding extra stock as needed to keep the fruit and nuts covered. You will not need it all. Remove the rabbit to a warmed serving dish, and pour the sauce over it. Garnish with lemon wedges if you wish.

NOTE Use 50 g/2 oz raisins instead of apricots if you wish.

SALAD MONTE CARLO
Serves 4–6

	UK	US as UK
49 g can anchovy fillets	$1\frac{3}{4}$ oz can	
30 ml oil	2 tbsp	
10–15 ml vinegar	2–3 tsp	
Pinch of dry mustard		
Salt and ground black pepper		
$\frac{1}{2}$ clove garlic		
Large leaves of 1 round lettuce		
3 medium tomatoes, cut into 8 segments each		
$\frac{1}{2}$ large green pepper, seeded and shredded		
1 small onion, cut into thin rings		
175 g cooked sliced green beans	6 oz	
225–275 g canned tuna in brine, drained OR cooked turkey meat without skin, cut into strips OR 125 g low fat hard cheese cut into small cubes	4 oz	
3 soaked prunes, stoned and cut into 4 pieces each		

Drain the anchovy fillets well, cut them in half lengthways and keep aside. Shake together in a screw-topped jar the oil, vinegar, mustard and a little salt and pepper. Crush or squeeze the garlic clove and add it to the jar. Lay the lettuce leaves flat, spread over a large platter.

Mix together the tomatoes, pepper, onion, and beans. Chop the tuna into small pieces if used; add the fish, meat or cheese to the vegetables. Shake the garlic dressing in the jar and toss the ingredients lightly in some or all of it. Spread them on the lettuce leaves in a flat, fairly thick layer. Arrange the anchovy fillets in a lattice pattern on top, and stick bits of prune, skin side up, in the spaces between.

NOTE You could use the oil from the can of anchovy fillets for the dressing.

MAIN DISHES
WITH CHEESE OR EGGS

WHOLEMEAL MACARONI CHEESE
Serves 4

	UK	US
175 g wholewheat macaroni or pasta shells	6 oz	2 cups
40 g low-fat spread	1½ oz	3 tbsp
40 g 100% or 85% wholemeal (whole wheat) flour	1½ oz	⅓ cup
575 ml skimmed milk	1 pt	2½ cups
125 g cooked bacon, luncheon meat or ham scraps from knuckle, chopped (optional – see note)	4 oz	½ cup
1 × 210 g can sweetcorn and peppers, drained	7 oz can	
125 g low-fat hard cheese, grated	4 oz	1 cup
Pinch of mustard powder		
Salt and freshly ground black pepper		
25 g whole-grain breadcrumbs	1 oz	4 tbsp

Break macaroni in short lengths. Cook either pasta in fast-boiling salted water, in a large pan, until tender. Drain well. Put the fat, flour and skimmed milk in a second large pan, over moderate heat, and whisk steadily until it boils and thickens. Add the meat if used (see note), the sweetcorn mix, 75 g/3 oz of the cheese, and the mustard and seasoning. Simmer for 2–3 minutes. Stir in the drained pasta, and pour the whole lot into a baking dish. Sprinkle with the breadcrumbs and the rest of the cheese. Bake at 200°C/400°F/Gas 6 for 20 minutes.

NOTE Use 125 g/4 oz cooked peas if you do not want to use meat or fish.

CHEESE-VEGETABLE FLAN
Serves 6

	UK	US
Recipe quantity wholemeal Shortcrust Pastry*		
125 g cooked fresh or frozen baby carrots, cut into small pieces	4 oz	
75 g cooked fresh or frozen green peas	3 oz	
150 g canned red kidney beans (one 213 g can, drained)	5 oz ($7\frac{1}{2}$ oz can)	
Salt and pepper		
25 g margarine	1 oz	2 tbsp
25 g white flour	1 oz	$\frac{1}{4}$ cup
125 g any hard cheese, grated	4 oz	1 cup

Place a 225 mm/9 in flan ring on a baking sheet (tray). Roll out the pastry and use it to line the ring. Re-roll any trimmings, and cut into narrow strips 5 mm/$\frac{1}{4}$ in wide and about 10 cm/4 in long. Lay them on the sheet beside the flan case. Heat the oven to 200°C/400°F/Gas 6. Line the pastry case with a sheet of greaseproof paper, and fill it with old dried beans. Bake it for 12–14 minutes until the top edge is lightly browned. Remove any narrow strips, and the beans and lining paper from the case. Return the case to the oven for 6–7 minutes to set the inside. Cool completely.

Drain the vegetables thoroughly, keeping them separate. Season lightly. Keep aside. (They should be well cooled.)

Melt the fat in a saucepan, stir in the flour, and continue stirring for 2 minutes. Off the heat, gradually stir in the milk without letting lumps form. Return to the heat, and bring to simmering point. Tip in the cheese, and stir until it melts. Cool, covered with damp greaseproof paper.

Spread the cheese sauce evenly in the flan case. Top with the vegetables in 3 separate segments radiating from the centre to the outer edge. Separate them with strips of pastry if you baked any. Serve cold.

BAKED STUFFED POTATOES
Serves 6

	UK	US
6 large old potatoes		

Oil for brushing
Stuffings
1)

	UK	US
75 g smoked haddock fillet, skinned, poached and flaked	3 oz	$\frac{1}{2}$ cup
15 ml chopped parsley	1 tbsp	
5 ml lemon juice	1 tsp	
5 ml milk	1 tsp	
Salt and pepper		

2)

	UK	US
50 g low-fat hard cheese, grated	2 oz	$\frac{1}{2}$ cup
15 g margarine	$\frac{1}{2}$ oz	1 tbsp
5 ml chopped parsley	1 tsp	
10 ml milk	2 tsp	
Salt and pepper		
2 egg yolks (stirred into stuffing)		
2 egg whites (beaten semi-stiff and folded in at the end)		

Scrub the potatoes, and brush with oil. Bake until tender at 190°C/375°F/Gas 5 ($1\frac{1}{4}$–$1\frac{1}{2}$ hours). Split in half lengthways and scoop out most of the inside into a bowl, leaving just a firm shell of skin and potato.

Mash the potato in the bowl, and mix with the chosen stuffing ingredients. Replace the mixture in the potato shells. EITHER bake for 15–20 minutes at the temperature above, or place under medium grilling heat to brown.

STUFFED COURGETTES (Zucchini)
Serves 2 or 3 as a main course, 6 as a starter or snack

	UK	US
3 courgettes (zucchini) about 125 g each	3 × 4 oz	
$\frac{1}{2}$ large onion, about 75 g skinned	3 oz	
$\frac{1}{2}$ green pepper, seeded		
15 ml oil	1 tbsp	
25 g oatmeal (fine if possible)	1 oz	2 tbsp
5 ml mixed dried herbs	1 tsp	
30 ml low fat hard cheese, or Cheddar cheese, grated	2 tbsp	
Salt and pepper (optional)		

150 ml Rosy Yoghurt Soup★ or		
Stabilised Yoghurt	$\frac{1}{4}$ pt	$\frac{1}{2}$ cup + 2 tbsp

Cut the stem ends off the courgettes (zucchini). Cook them for 5 minutes in boiling water. Drain and cool. Cut them in half lengthways, and scoop out most of the flesh with a pointed teaspoon. Keep the hollowed 'shells' aside. Cut up the flesh roughly.

Chop the onion and pepper together. Cook them gently in the oil in a frying pan (skillet) until just soft, stirring often. Add the courgette (zucchini) flesh, and sauté until the vegetables begin to brown. Take the pan off the heat. Mix in the oatmeal and dried herbs thoroughly, then the cheese. Season if you wish. Fill the mixture into the hollowed shells. Put them, cut side up, in a shallow baking dish. Trickle a little soup or yoghurt over each, and spoon the rest into the dish. Bake at 180°C/350°F/Gas 4 for 30 minutes or until the skins are soft. Eat hot or cold.

NOTE If courgettes (zucchini) are expensive or you cannot get them, use cooking pears. Blanch them for about 10 minutes before use.

PEANUT 'BURGERS
Makes 8 'burgers

	UK	US
575 ml skimmed milk	1 pt	$2\frac{1}{2}$ cups
125 g semolina	2 oz	$\frac{1}{3}$ cup
2.5 ml sea salt	$\frac{1}{2}$ tsp	
1.4 ml grated nutmeg	$\frac{1}{4}$ tsp	
10 ml finely chopped (minced) parsley	2 tsp	
2 eggs, beaten		
125 g wholemeal (whole wheat) flour	4 oz	1 cup
65 g salted peanuts, chopped	$2\frac{1}{2}$ oz	$\frac{1}{2}$ cup
15 g sesame seeds	$\frac{1}{2}$ oz	2 tsp
Corn oil for brushing		

Bring the milk to the boil in a fairly large pan over very low heat. Stir in the semolina, salt and nutmeg, and continue stirring until the mixture is very thick. Remove from the heat, and beat in the eggs, then all the other ingredients except the oil. Shape into eight patties about 6 cm/$2\frac{1}{2}$ in diameter. Place on an oiled baking tray and brush lightly with oil. Bake at 180°C/350°F/Gas 4 until lightly browned (about 30 minutes).

EGGS IN POTATO NESTS
Serves 4

	UK	US
600 g medium-sized potatoes, scrubbed	1¼ lb	
400 g medium-sized onions	¾ lb	
Salt		
25 g margarine	1 oz	2 tbsp
15 ml milk	1 tbsp	
Pepper		
Grated nutmeg		
4 eggs (size 3/medium)		

Scrub the potatoes and quarter them, or halve if small. Skin and slice the onions. Boil them together in slightly salted water until tender. Drain. Holding in a cloth, peel or scrape the potatoes. Mash them in a bowl with the onions, fat, milk, a little seasoning and the nutmeg. Spread in a 3–4 cm/1–1½ in layer all over a shallow baking dish, and level the top. Make 4 hollows in the mixture, and smooth the potato taken out over the rest. Keep warm under greased paper or foil. Poach the eggs, and slide one into each hollow. Sprinkle very lightly with extra seasoning and nutmeg. Serve at once.

DISHES FOR LIGHT AND SNACK MEALS

ROSY YOGHURT SOUP
Single helping(s)

	UK	US
150 ml natural yoghurt	¼ pt	½ cup + 2 tbsp
60 ml tomato juice	4 tbsp	
5 ml orange juice	1 tsp	
Grinding of black pepper (optional)		

Beat all the ingredients in a jug until smooth. Chill in a refrigerator if possible, until thickened, or cool in a pan of cold water. Drink as a light quick meal-in-a-cup, or as a summer soup. Also makes a good dip.

TARATOR LUNCH
Single helping(s)

	UK	US
½ cut garlic clove (optional)		
6.5 cm or 75 g cucumber	2½ in or 3 oz	
6–8 leaves of fresh mint		
1 spring onion (scallion) green and white parts, sliced		
150 ml natural yoghurt	¼ pt	½ cup + 2 tbsp
Salt		
Pinch of sugar (optional)		
1 hard-boiled (hard-cooked) egg, finely chopped (optional)		

Rub the cut side of the garlic around the inside of a soup bowl or cup if you like garlic, and have a clove to use up. Shred or chop the cucumber, mint and spring onion; do them all together if you have a food mill. Beat in the yoghurt and a little salt.

Add a pinch of sugar if the yoghurt is sour. Fold in the hard-boiled egg if you use it: it makes a satisfying meal. Chill well before serving (stand the bowl in very cold water for some time if you have no fridge). Eat with crispbread.

This dish also makes a good 'starter' for a family meal or dinner-party. If you use the egg, this quantity will serve 2 people.

SHAPELY TOMATO CUPS
Serves 4

	UK	US
8 small firm tomatoes, 50 g wgt each	8 fruit, 2 oz wgt each	As UK
90 ml low-fat soft cheese	6 tbsp	
20 ml low-fat spread	4 tsp	
2 hard-boiled (hard-cooked) eggs (Size 3/medium)		
10 ml chopped parsley	2 tsp	
Salt and pepper		
Extra low-fat soft cheese for garnish (optional)		
Shredded lettuce		

Cut the tomatoes in half, remove the seeds and pulp, and turn upside-down to drain. (Add the seeds and pulp to a stew or soup.)

Blend the low-fat soft cheese with the spread in a soup plate or shallow bowl. Chop up the eggs and mash them into the cheese with the parsley. Season lightly.

Fill the mixture into the tomato halves. If you wish, pipe a rosette of extra soft cheese on top of each tomato half. Arrange on shredded lettuce. Serve cold as a first course or snack meal, with fingers of hot dry toast (the filling tastes richer than it is).

For ONE PERSON, make half the quantity of cheese mixture, and use it for 2 snack meals. Serve half of it in 2 tomato halves, and the other half the following day piled on a slice of wholemeal bread.

HI-FI SANDWICHES
Makes 4 sandwiches

	UK	US
8 slices of high-bran bread		
Filling 1		
50 g low-fat soft cheese	2 oz	$\frac{1}{4}$ cup
10 ml low-fat spread	2 tsp	
A few drops of Worcestershire sauce		
15 ml grated carrot or chopped parsley	1 tbsp	
2 hard-boiled (hard-cooked) eggs		
Filling 2		
1 213 g can red kidney beans	$7\frac{1}{2}$ oz can	
20 ml low-fat soft cheese	4 tsp	
10 ml tomato chutney (sweet pickle)	2 tsp	

For Filling 1, mix the cheese and low-fat spread in a bowl, and blend in the Worcestershire sauce. Mix in the carrot or parsley. Shell the eggs, chop them and mash them into the cheese mixture. Pile on 4 slices of bread and cover with 4 more slices.

For Filling 2, drain the beans, then mash all the ingredients together. Spread on 4 slices of bread, and cover with 4 more slices.

NOTE You can add a little shredded lettuce to the sandwiches before covering them if you wish.

LIVER SPREAD ROLLS
Serves 4–6

	UK	US
4 large or 6 small wholemeal or high-bran rolls		
125 g soft liver sausage or spread	4 oz	$\frac{1}{2}$ cup
1 medium-sized tomato		
75 g low-fat soft cheese or curd cheese	3 oz	
5 ml chopped parsley	1 tsp	
Margarine (if serving hot)		

Split the rolls. Take any plastic 'skin' off the liver sausage or spread.

Quarter the tomato, take out the seeds, and chop the flesh. Mix it with the sausage or spread. Spread this mixture on the bottom halves of the rolls. Mix the cheese and parsley, and spread on the top halves of the rolls. Reassemble the rolls. Chill or leave in a cold place, covered, if for use later as a packed or snack meal.

If you wish, place the rolls on a well-greased baking sheet (tray). Dot the tops with margarine. Heat in the oven at 160°C/325°F/Gas 3 for 8–10 minutes.

SAVOURY BEANBURGERS
Makes 4

	UK	US as UK
One 450 g can baked beans in tomato sauce	15.9 oz can	
75 g low-fat hard cheese, grated or crumbled	3 oz	
125 g soft white or wholemeal breadcrumbs or a mixture	4 oz	
4 round soft rolls		
Extra low-fat hard cheese for sprinkling		

Drain the beans thoroughly, and keep the sauce aside. Mash the beans to break them up, and mix with the cheese and breadcrumbs. Shape into 4 flat round patties. Place under a hot grill and cook, turning once, until golden on each side. While cooking, split the rolls. Remove the 'burgers and toast the cut sides of the rolls lightly. Put in the 'burgers, top with extra cheese and a little of the sauce, and reshape the rolls. Serve at once.

(Use the rest of the sauce for another dish.)

LENTIL AND CELERY PATTIES
Serves 4

	UK	US
275 g cooked red lentils (page 20)	10 oz	
125 g walnut pieces or chopped mixed nuts	4 oz	1 cup
3 celery stalks		
150 g soft wholemeal or high-bran breadcrumbs	5 oz	2 cups

15 ml chopped parsley	1 tbsp
1 medium-sized onion, finely chopped	
30 ml oil	2 tbsp
Salt and ground black pepper	
5 ml lemon juice (optional)	1 tsp

Mash the lentils to a coarse paste. Grind the nuts to a coarse powder in a nut mill or mincer (grinder) without letting them oil. Chop the celery finely. Mix all these ingredients in a bowl with the breadcrumbs. Fry the chopped onion in the oil until just soft, and add to the bowl with the remaining oil. Season. Mix well. Taste and add the lemon juice if you wish. Shape into 8 small patties or 4 large ones, and leave to stand for 30 minutes. Oil a baking sheet, and bake the patties at 190°C/375°F/Gas 5 for 20–35 minutes, depending on the size of the patties. Serve hot with chopped, simmered tomatoes, flavoured with lemon juice and chopped parsley.

MACKEREL KEBABS
Single helping

	UK	US
1 198 g can mackerel steaks in brine (3 or 4 pieces fish)	7 oz can	As UK
3 or 4 button mushrooms (optional)		
22 ml honey	1½ tbsp	
15 ml lemon juice	1 tbsp	
5 ml Worcestershire sauce	1 tsp	
Small pinch of dry mustard		
½ medium onion, skinned		
1 tomato		

Drain the mackerel steaks, and put in a bowl with the mushrooms if used. Put the honey, lemon juice, Worcestershire sauce and mustard in a saucepan, and warm them, stirring, until the honey melts. Pour over the mackerel and mushrooms. Leave for 20 minutes, turning occasionally. Cut onion into pieces and slice the tomato across into 3 or 4 thick rounds.

Thread the mackerel, mushroom, onion and tomato alternatively on one or two thin skewers. Sprinkle with sauce mixture. Grill (broil) turning once or twice and sprinkling with sauce, for 7–8 minutes.

NOTE This quantity would make 2 snack meals if you have a small appetite. You could leave half the ingredients in a refrigerator, and eat them as a salad next day (without the onion).

SEAFOOD TOWERS (mini-salad open sandwiches)
Serves 2

	UK	US as UK
1 small egg		
One 220 g can tuna in brine or sardines	$7\frac{1}{2}$ oz can	
20 ml mayonnaise or thick Milk Salad Dressing*	4 tsp	
2.5 ml tomato ketchup (catsup)	$\frac{1}{2}$ tsp	
1 medium-sized tomato		
Salt and pepper		
2 soft-topped rolls or 'burger buns		

Ahead of time, hard-boil (hard-cook) the egg and cool it. Drain the canned fish, and mash with the mayonnaise or dressing and ketchup. Cut the tomato across in half and cut off the ends to make 2 thick rounds. Season them well.

Cut the tops off the rolls or buns (use as crumbs for another dish). Pile the fish mixture on the cut sides, and flatten the top of each pile. Put one round of tomato on each pile. Shell the egg, cut it in half across, and place a half egg, cut side down, on each round of tomato like a tall hat.

NOTE For a packed meal, top the tomato rounds with the tops of the rolls instead of the egg.

EGG SALAD NESTS
Single helping

	UK	US as UK
1 hard-boiled (hard-cooked) egg		
50 g white cabbage	2 oz	
$\frac{1}{2}$ small carrot		
25 g mild Dutch cheese or low-fat hard cheese	1 oz	
10 ml sultanas (golden raisins)	2 tsp	
10 ml mayonnaise or to taste	2 tsp	

145

5–10 ml chutney (sweet pickle)   1–2 tsp
Salt and pepper

Shell the egg. Shred the cabbage, carrot and cheese finely, and mix with
the sultanas. Combine the mayonnaise and chutney, and use to bind the
mixture, without hiding the shreds. Season. Put the slaw in an individual
bowl, and make a hollow in the centre, into which you put the egg. Eat
with hot toast or crispbread.

VEGETABLES

DUCHESS POTATOES
Makes 700 g/1½ lb (approx)

	UK	US
700 g old potatoes	1½ lb	
40 g margarine	1½ oz	3 tbsp
1 whole egg, beaten with:		
1 egg yolk		
Salt and pepper		
Margarine for greasing		
Beaten egg or egg white for glazing		

Scrub the potatoes, and boil or steam them until tender. Drain. Scrape them, cutting off any scabbed or tough skin. Sieve them into a bowl, and beat in the margarine and eggs. Season. Grease a baking sheet. Pipe or shape spoonfuls of the mixture into rounds or rosettes on the sheet. Brush with beaten egg or egg white. Bake at 200°C/400°F/Gas 6 for about 15 minutes or until the potato is firm and tipped with brown.

NOTE The potato mixture can be made ahead of time, shaped and frozen.

BAKED CASSEROLED POTATOES
Serves 4–6

	UK	US as UK
450 g tomatoes	1 lb	
225 g onions	8 oz	
15 ml oil	1 tbsp	
2.5 ml salt	½ tsp	
Good pinch of black pepper		
2.5 ml chopped fresh or dried basil	½ tsp	

147

2.5 ml chopped fresh or dried thyme	$\frac{1}{2}$ tsp	
1 large clove garlic		
900 g boiling potatoes	2 lb	

Slice the tomatoes. Slice the onions thinly and put them in a pan with the oil. Simmer them over low heat, stirring until they are just softened. Off the heat, mix in the sliced tomatoes. Add the seasonings and chopped herbs. Squeeze the garlic over the mixture.

Peel the potatoes if the skins are coarse and old; just scrub or scrape new or thin-skinned potatoes. Slice them 3 mm/$\frac{1}{8}$ in thick.

Spread about a quarter of the onion-tomato mixture over the bottom of an oiled, shallow baking dish about 250 mm/10 in in diameter and 50–75 mm/2–3 in deep. Cover with half the potato slices in an even layer. Spread about half the remaining tomato-onion over the potatoes. Repeat the potato layer, using all the slices and top with the last of the tomato-onion mixture.

Cover loosely with greased foil and bake at 200°C/400°F/Gas 6 for about 1$\frac{1}{4}$ hours. Remove the foil for the last 15 minutes.

PORTUGUESE VEGETABLES
Serves 4

	UK	US
450 g courgettes (zucchini) or peeled aubergine (eggplant) (see note 1)	1 lb	
1 large onion, skinned and chopped		
1 garlic clove, peeled and chopped		
25 g low-fat spread or margarine	1 oz	2 tbsp
4 medium tomatoes, about 350 g in all, or 1 × 410 g can tomatoes, drained	12 oz or 14 oz can	
30 ml tomato purée	2 tbsp	
5 ml dried thyme	1 tsp	
45 ml water (see note 2)	3 tbsp	
A little salt and ground black pepper		

Cut the unpeeled courgettes (zucchini) into 1 cm/$\frac{1}{2}$ in slices, discarding the ends, or cut the aubergine (eggplant) into 2 cm/$\frac{3}{4}$ in cubes. In a large frying pan or flameproof baking dish, stir the onion and garlic in the fat over a low heat until they soften. Add the sliced or cubed vegetable, and stir for 3–4 minutes. Leave to simmer while you slice the tomatoes, and mix the tomato purée and dried thyme into the water. Add the sliced tomatoes to the dish and season lightly, then mix in the liquid. Turn the whole lot into a shallow baking dish, and cover with greased foil or a lid. Bake at 180°C/350°F/Gas 4 for 30–40 minutes.

NOTES

1) You can mix 1 or 2 courgettes (zucchini) with 1 medium-sized aubergine (eggplant), to make up the weight of vegetables, or you can substitute other vegetables if cheaper. Try blanched cauliflower sprigs and cubed potato.

2) If you want a dish with a sauce, add 2–3 spoonfuls more water or the end of a bottle of wine, when mixing with the purée.

3) You can bake and serve the vegetables over fish steaks or cover them with 275 ml/$\frac{1}{2}$ pt (1$\frac{1}{4}$ cups) Cheese Sauce* just before serving.

MIXED VEGETABLES IN A POTATO RING
Serves 6

	UK	US
700 g Duchess potato mixture (see p.147)	1$\frac{1}{2}$ lb	
700 g mixed parsnips, turnips, carrots, leeks, cauliflower, or frozen mixed vegetables	1$\frac{1}{2}$ lb	
25 g margarine	1 oz	2 tbsp
150 ml boiling water	$\frac{1}{4}$ pt	$\frac{1}{2}$ cup + 2 tbsp
Salt and pepper		
Good pinch of dried mixed herbs		
250 g cooked, or canned, drained cannellini beans (1 × 425 g can)	9 oz or one 15 oz can	

Prepare the Duchess potato mixture or thaw it if frozen. Prepare the vegetables. If using fresh vegetables, slice the roots and leeks thinly, and break the cauliflower into florets. Melt the fat in a fairly large saucepan, add the root vegetables and cover the pan. Shake or toss the vegetables over moderate heat; add the cauliflower sprigs after about 3 minutes, then the leeks. Toss briefly, then add the boiling water, a little salt and the thyme. Cover, lower the heat, and simmer until the vegetables are almost tender. Add the beans, and continue cooking until heated through.

If using frozen, mixed vegetables, toss them in the fat until melted, then add the water, salt and thyme. Simmer, covered for a few minutes only, then add the beans and heat through.

While simmering the vegetables, pipe or shape the Duchess potato mixture into a ring about 225 mm/9 in across. Bake at 200°C/400°F/Gas 6 for 12–15 minutes until lightly browned. Drain the vegetables, season lightly with salt and pepper and pile in the centre of the ring. Serve hot.

VEGETABLES A LA GRECQUE
Serves 6 as a starter or 4 as a main vegetarian dish

For 450 g/1 lb prepared vegetables, use:

	UK	US
1 garlic clove, skinned		
350 g tomatoes, chopped	12 oz	
30 ml lemon juice	2 tbsp	
60 ml oil	4 tbsp	
175 ml water	6 fl oz	$\frac{3}{4}$ cup
1 bay leaf		
1.5 ml ground coriander	$\frac{1}{4}$ tsp	
Salt and pepper		
450 g vegetables (see below)	1 lb	

Vegetables à la Grecque are good hot or cold, as a starter or as a vegetable with, or instead of, a main dish. They also make an excellent dressing for plain meat or fish, e.g. over chicken joints, white fish fillet. Leeks, mushrooms, cauliflower, aubergine, artichokes (Jerusalem), celeriac, green beans or onions, are all good à la Grecque.

Squeeze the garlic clove over the tomatoes. Put all the remaining ingredients in a pan, and bring to the boil. Add the garlic and tomatoes. Half-cover and cook gently for 20 minutes, then cover and boil fairly fast for another 10 minutes until most of the liquid has evaporated. While cooking, add the prepared vegetables when appropriate. Raw vegetables which you want to serve cooked should be cut into small enough pieces to cook through in 20 minutes and should be cooked in the sauce. Serve hot or cold. Cooked vegetables or ones to be served raw should be added to the sauce for the last 5 minutes of the cooking time for serving hot; for serving cold, simply steep them in the hot sauce until it cools.

SHORT-COOKED CARROTS AND BEANS

Serves 2–3

	UK	US as UK
125 g young carrots	4 oz	
125 g frozen sliced green beans	4 oz	
125 g onion, skinned and chopped	4 oz	
30 ml chopped parsley	2 tbsp	
60 ml water	4 tbsp	
15 ml margarine	1 tbsp	
Salt and freshly ground black pepper		

Top and tail the carrots, and scrape if needed. Cut them across into very thin rounds like potato crisps. Cut the beans in half if long. Put the vegetables and parsley in a saucepan with the water and fat. Bring to the boil, and cook gently, covered, for 5–7 minutes or until the carrots and onions are tender. Season lightly and serve with any remaining liquid.

POLISH BROAD BEANS

Serves 2–3

	UK	US
275 g frozen broad beans	10 oz	
10 ml honey	2 tsp	
5 ml yellow French mustard	1 tsp	
150 ml Stabilised Yoghurt★	¼ pt	½ cup + 2 tbsp
30 ml soft wholemeal breadcrumbs	2 tbsp	

Simmer the beans until tender (8–9 minutes). Drain well, and turn into a shallow ovenproof dish. Warm the honey, and mix in the mustard, then mix both with the yoghurt. Pour the mixture over the beans. Sprinkle with the crumbs. Put in the oven at 180°C/350°F/Gas 4, covered with lightly greased foil. Bake for 10–12 minutes or until well heated through. Serve with bacon or beefburgers as a main dish for 2, or alone as a side dish for 2–3.

SALADS

SPINACH SALAD
Serves 3–4

	UK	US
225 g young fresh spinach	8 oz	
2 large spring onions (scallions), green and white parts		
150 g fresh tomato, chopped in biggish pieces (1 fairly big tomato)	5 oz	
Dressing		
150 ml natural yoghurt	$\frac{1}{4}$ pt	$\frac{1}{2}$ cup + 2 tbsp
10 ml lemon juice	2 tsp	
5 ml oil	1 tsp	
$\frac{1}{2}$ garlic clove, squeezed over yoghurt		
1.5 ml dried thyme	$\frac{1}{4}$ tsp	

Tear out the ribs of the spinach leaves, then tear the leaves into small pieces. Slice the spring onions (scallions) on the diagonal. Add them with the tomato to the leaves in a salad bowl. Mix together all the dressing ingredients until blended, then pour it over the salad and toss by hand until well mixed in. Serve at once.

NOTE No salt and pepper is needed.

GREEN BEAN SALAD
Serves 2–3

	UK	US as UK
1 medium-sized onion		
225 g fresh or frozen green beans, sliced if thick	8 oz	

152

	UK	US
30 ml oil	2 tbsp	
15 ml lemon juice	1 tbsp	
Salt and pepper		

Slice the onion into very thin rings. Cook the beans in fresh water until just tender, adding the onion for the last 4–5 minutes. While cooking, mix together the oil, lemon juice and seasonings in a jug. Whisk well to blend. Drain the vegetables as soon as the beans are tender. Toss in the dressing while still warm. Cool before use.

APPLE AND CELERY SALAD
Serves 3–4

	UK	US
3 small red-skinned apples		
1 small cooking apple		
15 ml orange juice	1 tbsp	
5 ml lemon juice	1 tsp	
2 celery stalks		
50 g salted peanuts	2 oz	$\frac{1}{3}$ cup
Ground black pepper		
15 ml grated orange rind	1 tsp	
75 ml mayonnaise	3 fl oz	$\frac{1}{3}$ cup

Core the apples without peeling them, chop them and toss in the orange and lemon juice. Slice the celery stalks thinly, and chop the nuts.

Mix the apples with the celery and half the nuts. Season with pepper, and 5 ml/1 tsp orange rind.

Crush the rest of the nuts finely. Mix together the crushed nuts, mayonnaise and remaining orange rind. Pile the salad on individual plates, and spoon the nut dressing over each helping.

BANANA AND CELERY SALAD
Serves 2

	UK	US as UK
1 medium-sized banana		
1 long stalk celery		
12–18 drained capers		
30 ml Milk Salad Dressing*	2 tbsp	

Peel and slice the banana. Chop the celery stalk. Mix with the banana and capers in a bowl, then fold in the dressing.

NOTE For a main course dish, top with any crumbly cheese, or dryish curd or pot cheese.

CARROT, PEPPER AND ORANGE SALAD
Serves 2
2 medium-sized carrots
½ large green pepper
1 small orange
Salt and ground black pepper
1 shallot or 2 spring onions (scallions)

Slice the carrots thickly. Core and de-seed the pepper if needed. Peel the orange and cut it up, to expose the pips. Remove them. Season these ingredients well. Put them all in a food processor and chop them, not too finely, or put them through a mincer (grinder), using the coarse holes. The orange should supply enough juice to be a dressing.

Separately, slice the shallot or onions very thinly, and mix into the coarsely chopped salad.

NOTE If the orange does not supply enough juice, add a little from a carton.

THREE BEAN SALAD
Serves 6

	UK	US
250 g cooked haricot or cannellini beans or 1 × 425 g can, drained	9 oz or 15 oz can	1½ cups
250 g cooked red kidney beans or 1 × 425 g can, drained	9 oz or 15 oz can	1½ cups
275 g cooked green beans (fresh or frozen)	9 oz	
15 ml fresh herbs, finely chopped (minced) – optional, see note	1 tbsp	
Lemon juice or natural yoghurt		
Salt and ground black pepper		

Mix the beans in a salad bowl, making sure they are well drained.

Sprinkle with herbs, and toss with a little lemon juice or yoghurt (not enough to coat them); season.

NOTE If you have not got a plot or window box of fresh herbs and cannot buy them, use a thinly sliced small onion, blanched and chopped, or the green parts of 1 or 2 spring onions (scallions).

WINTER (OR SUMMER) SLAW
Serves 4

	UK	US
¼ white cabbage (about 350 g)	12 oz	
50 g ready-to-use dried apricots, or raisins	2 oz	¼ cup
1 red-skinned apple		
50 g salted peanuts	2 oz	⅓ cup
5 ml celery seeds	1 tsp	
150 ml natural yoghurt or yoghurt with pineapple	¼ pt	½ cup + 2 tbsp

Chop or shred the cabbage finely. Chop the apricots if used. Core and chop the apple. Mix the cabbage, apricots or raisins, chopped apple, peanuts and celery seeds in a bowl. Mix in the yoghurt until well blended. Serve cold.

NOTE An attractive sweetish slaw can be made by using extra-low fat black cherry yoghurt.

SIMPLE SLAW WITH PROTEIN DRESSING
Serves 2

	UK	US
125 g (¼ small) red or firm white cabbage	4 oz	
2 spring onions (scallions) green and white parts		
½ green pepper		
15 ml mayonnaise	1 tbsp	
15 ml water	1 tbsp	
125 g long-life tofu, drained or mild low fat soft cheese	4 oz	½ cup

Chop the cabbage, spring onions and pepper roughly. Then shred them together or mince (grind) them, using the coarse mesh on the machine. Beat the mayonnaise and water together, or shake them in the bottle if you have a spoonful left in one. Beat the tofu or cheese until smooth and creamy, then beat in the diluted mayonnaise. Use to bind the salad ingredients.

RIBBON SALAD IDEAS

The idea of a ribbon salad is that you keep the ingredients separate, and arrange them in lines across your plate or dish. Season and dress them separately first if they need it; for instance you will need to dip chopped apple in fruit juice or French dressing to prevent it turning brown, or you may want to sprinkle grated raw carrot with lemon or orange juice. Put ingredients with contrasting colours next to each other. White beans will not show up against cauliflower sprigs.

Use as many raw ingredients as you can; some foods have to be blanched, or cooked and cooled, but they do lose value in the process.

If you eat alone, a vivid small plateful of ribbon salad can give you a dish as pretty as a posy, just as easy to prepare as a mixed salad in a bowl, and even easier to eat. If you have a family or a party to cater for, a large ribbon salad gives you a splashy, colourful, rich-looking dish for no more trouble and expense than two or three small bowls. Here are some ideas.

1) A centre line of drained canned sweetcorn, flanked on each side by small blanched mushrooms; beside the mushrooms, put lines of chopped sweet red pepper, and make outside lines of sliced, blanched leeks.
NOTE Blanch mushrooms for 3 minutes in water flavoured with Worcestershire sauce. Simmer leek slices for about 4 minutes, in water flavoured with lemon juice.

2) Use a centre line of cooked brown rice. Flank with lines of cooked, cooled peas. Flank the peas with 2 lines of sliced raw tomato, and border with finely chopped celery.

3) Make the centre line chopped or coarsely grated raw carrot mixed with grated orange rind; flank with chopped hard-boiled (hard-cooked) egg or cottage cheese; beside this, put blanched mushrooms for black-white contrast, border with shredded lettuce, green cabbage or spinach.

4) Centre line blanched cauliflower sprigs, fresh or frozen; second line, drained canned red kidney beans; third line, chopped unpeeled red apple dipped in lemon juice or dressing; fourth line (optional), small cooked Brussels sprouts.

SOME COLOUR CHOICES

White Cauliflower sprigs, chopped hard-boiled (hard-cooked) egg white, cooked cubed turnip, raw or blanched beansprouts, haricot or butter (navy) beans, finely sliced raw onion or spring onions (scallions), new potatoes.

Yellow or cream Sweetcorn kernels, sliced banana, chopped canned pineapple, fresh or canned yellow peach slices, sweet yellow peppers; cooked cubed swede (rutabaga); lightly curried rice, grated hard cheese.

Orange or peach Carrot, rose-fleshed melon cubes, cubed or mashed cooked pumpkin, chopped fresh or canned apricots.

Red or purple Shredded red cabbage, cooked beetroot, sliced tomatoes, red radishes, red kidney beans, unpeeled red plums, sweet red peppers, stoned halved cherries, strawberries, raspberries.

Black or dark brown Black or dark brown cooked beans (various), cooked mushrooms, stoned black olives, soaked, stoned chopped prunes, pickled walnuts, blackcurrants, pipped black grapes.

Green All the green leaf vegetables, e.g. spinach, various lettuces, Chinese leaves, kale; broccoli, Brussels sprouts, green beans (various), flageolet (lima) beans, garden peas, cucumber, courgettes (zucchini), green-flesh melon, all herbs, e.g. parsley sprigs, green onion tops.

PLAIN AND SWEET BAKED GOODS

CRUMB PASTRY

Makes one 200 mm/8 in flan ring or tart shell

NOTE Americans should note that in this recipe, the term *biscuit* means any dry crisp cookie or wafer, not the type of baked goods used for shortcakes etc.

	UK	US
225 g biscuit crumbs (see below)	8 oz	2 cups
Up to 30 ml finely chopped or grated nuts or cheese, unsweetened dessicated coconut, seeds, herbs or ground spices, etc	up to 2 tbsp	
75–100 g margarine or other fat (see recipe)	3–4 oz	$\frac{1}{3}-\frac{1}{2}$ cup
Up to 50 g sweetening if for a sweet dish – to taste	up to 2 oz	

Any biscuit crumbs, crispbread crumbs or crushed breakfast cereal can be used, to suit the chosen filling. Crush by rolling with a rolling pin or bottle between 2 sheets of greaseproof or waxed paper. The crumbs should be fine and even. Mix in any dry flavourings, adjusting the quantity to suit your taste and the type of crumbs, e.g. 5 ml/1 tsp ground ginger may be enough with ginger biscuit crumbs but 30 ml/2 tbsp mild grated cheese will be needed with cracker crumbs. Prepare a flan case or tart (pie) case by greasing. Line with paper and grease the inside of the lining if the crumb pastry case will be removed from the container.

Melt or soften and blend the fat and any sweetening together. Margarine is the usual fat, but vegetable fat or soft cheese could be used for a savoury case. Adjust the quantity to suit the type of crumbs. Dry cracker crumbs may need extra fat. Mix the fat into the crumbs thoroughly.

Press the crumbs firmly all over the inside of the prepared case, making the sides thick and even. Prepare these first and trim the top rim with a knife held flat so that loose crumbs fall into the crumb shell and can be pressed into the base. Chill and use the case as it is; or bake it at 160°C/ 325°F/Gas 3 for 15–20 minutes to firm it up, if the filling will be wet. Use warm or cold.

WHOLEMEAL BREAD 'CARRIERS'

1) *Tartlet Cases* Use thin round slices of bread, cut out with a pastry cutter from large square slices of a tin (pan) loaf. Using a pastry brush, dab the slices on one side with melted margarine. Then press them gently, greased side *down*, into individual bun tins (muffin pans), baking dishes or tartlet tins (pans). Dab the inside surfaces with a little more melted fat. Then bake at 180°C/350°F/Gas 4 for 15–20 minutes until crisp and golden brown. Turn out, cool, and use like tartlet cases baked 'blind'.

2) *Canapé Carriers* Use slightly stale bread, and cut it in slices 5 mm/ $\frac{1}{4}$ in thick; very thin slices are brittle or sag. Cut off the crusts, then toast the slices on both sides. They are easier to cut into neat shapes if toasted before cutting. Cut into rounds, triangles or fingers.

If you prefer, you can bake the 'carriers'. Cut out the shapes you want, then dab them with melted margarine. Place them on a greased baking sheet, and bake like tartlet cases.

Squares, triangles and fingers are best cut out with scissors. Rounds can be cut out with a pastry cutter.

BASIC NO-KNEAD BREAD
Makes three 850 g/1$\frac{3}{4}$ lb loaves

	UK	US
700 g plain wholemeal (whole wheat) flour (see note 1)	1$\frac{1}{2}$ lb	6 cups
700 g strong white flour (see note 1)	1$\frac{1}{2}$ lb	6 cups
10 ml salt	2 tsp	
1.0–1.1 L lukewarm water	1$\frac{3}{4}$–2 pt	2$\frac{1}{4}$–2$\frac{1}{2}$ pt
22 ml dried yeast with vitamin C or as packet instructions direct	2 tbsp	
15 ml honey	1 tbsp	

159

Mix the flours and salt in a large mixing bowl. Put 1.1 L/2 pt hand-hot water in a jug. Mix the dry yeast into the flour, and stir the honey into the water in the jug.

Add the sweetened water slowly to the flour, working it in with a wooden spoon first, then with your hands, until you have a smooth dough which leaves the sides of the bowl cleanly. You probably will not need all the water (see Note 1); it will depend on the quality and condition of the flour.

Sprinkle the surface of the dough with a little extra flour, and lift the sides into the middle to make a ball of dough without creases. Turn it onto a board and pat into a rectangle. Leave to stand while you grease three 75 mm/3 in deep bread tins (pans) (225 × 125 mm/9 × 5 in approx.). Cut the dough into three equal-sized oblongs. Place one in each tin (pan) and level the tops. Leave in a fairly warm place until the dough almost reaches the tops of the containers; meanwhile heat the oven to 200°C/400°F/Gas 6. Bake the loaves for 35–40 minutes or until they sound hollow when tapped on the bottom. Cool on a wire rack before cutting.

NOTES

1) You can vary the proportions of the two flours if you wish; if you can get strong wholemeal flour, try using wholemeal only. The more wholemeal flour you use, the more water you are likely to need. This will affect the weight of your loaves.

2) Vitamin C is sometimes called ascorbic acid or bread improver. Dried yeast with vitamin C may vary in performance, so if instructions for its use are given on the packet, follow them.

3) If you wish, brush the tops of risen loaves lightly with milk before baking, omitting the edges, and sprinkle with sesame seeds, celery seeds or caraway seeds.

4) An attractive variation is to add 4 ml/1$\frac{3}{4}$ tsp ground mixed spice to one loaf. Brush the top with water when risen and sprinkle lightly with spice and sugar mixed. (Use in proportions of 5 ml/1 tsp sugar to 1.5 ml/$\frac{1}{4}$ tsp spice.)

QUICK OATEN BREAD
Makes one 900 g/2 lb loaf

	UK	US
300 g plain wholemeal (whole wheat) flour	11 oz	3 cups
300 g strong white flour	11 oz	3 cups
50 g porridge oats	2 oz	$\frac{2}{3}$ cup
5 ml bicarbonate of soda (baking soda)	1 tsp	
5 ml salt	1 tsp	
50 g softened margarine	2 oz	$\frac{1}{4}$ cup
425 ml sour milk	$\frac{3}{4}$ pt	2 cups
Margarine for greasing		
Sour milk and porridge oats for topping		

Mix both flours, the oats, soda and salt in a large bowl. Beat in the fat. Then mix in the milk slowly, with a wooden spoon, to make a soft but not wet dough; you may need a very little more milk. Knead for 2–3 minutes by hand to mix in all the dry goods. Grease a loaf tin (pan) well (230 × 125 × 75 mm/9 × 5 × 3 in is a good size). Turn in the dough, press down into the corners and level the top with your hand. Brush lightly with milk, avoiding the edges. Sprinkle with oats. Bake at 200°C/400°F/Gas 6 for 50–60 minutes; when ready the loaf will sound hollow if tapped on the bottom. Cool on a wire rack if possible. Leave for 4 hours before cutting, to prevent the bread being 'sad' (heavy); this happens if it cools too fast through the steam escaping.

NOTE The American quantities in this recipe are very slightly larger but fit the same sized tin (pan).

QUICK SOYA BREAD OR ROLLS
Makes one 700 g/1$\frac{1}{2}$ lb loaf

	UK	US
225 g wholemeal (whole wheat) self-raising flour	8 oz	2 cups
225 g white self-raising flour	8 oz	2 cups
50 g soya flour	2 oz	$\frac{1}{2}$ cup
5 ml salt	1 tsp	
5 ml baking powder	1 tsp	
50 g margarine	2 oz	$\frac{1}{4}$ cup
275 ml milk or water	$\frac{1}{2}$ pt	1$\frac{1}{4}$ cups

Grease a loaf tin about 190 × 115 mm/7½ × 4½ in in size, and 75 mm/3 in deep. Sift together the three flours, salt and baking powder into a bowl, and return any bran in the sifter to the mixture. Rub in the fat, then mix in the milk or water. Knead for 2 minutes, or until the dough is smooth and uncreased. Turn it into the tin, making sure it fills the corners, and level the top. Make 3 diagonal slashes on the top of the loaf. Bake at 220°C/425°F/Gas 7 for 30 minutes or until risen and golden-brown. It should sound hollow when tapped on the bottom. Cool on a wire rack, and store closely wrapped for not more than 48 hours.

If you prefer, shape the mixture into 10 round or oval rolls. Bake for 20 minutes.

MUSHROOM BREAD
Makes one 900 g/2 lb loaf

	UK	US
125 ml milk	4 fl oz	½ cup
15 ml margarine	1 tbsp	
1.5 ml salt	¼ tsp	
30 ml plain dried yeast	2 tbsp	
175 ml lukewarm water	6 fl oz	¾ cup
15 ml sugar	1 tbsp	
400 g wholemeal (whole wheat) flour	14 oz	3½ cups
125 g strong white flour	4 oz	1 cup
125 g button mushrooms	4 oz	
10 ml dried sliced onions, soaked	2 tsp	

Put the milk in a small saucepan with the fat and salt. Bring it to simmering point, then remove from the heat and cool to lukewarm. Sprinkle the yeast into the warm water and sugar in a large mixing bowl, and leave until creamy and bubbling. Sift the two flours together onto stout paper; return any bran in the sifter to the mixture. Put 50 g/2 oz of the flour aside. Stir the milk mixture into the yeast liquid, then gradually stir in the flour and bran mixture. Knead by hand to a firm dough, adding a little more water if needed. Then turn onto a lightly floured surface, and knead until the dough is elastic.

Oil the inside of the bowl, put in the dough, and turn it over to film it with oil. Cover loosely, and leave in a warm place until well risen and puffy. Meanwhile, chop the mushrooms finely, drain the onions and mix them together.

Mix the mushrooms and onions by spoonfuls into the risen dough. (It will make the mixture sticky.) Scatter half the reserved flour onto a clean surface, and use it to make the dough firm again. You may not need it all. Knead again for about 5 minutes.

Grease a 225 × 125 × 75 mm/9 × 5 × 3 in loaf tin (pan). Shape the dough into a smooth oblong, and put it into the tin. Grease the top if you wish. Leave in a warm place for 45 minutes or until the dough fills the tin (pan). Bake at 200°C/400°F/Gas 6 for 40 minutes or until the loaf sounds hollow when tapped on the bottom. Cool on a wire rack, or balanced across the top of the pan.

STEAMED GOLDEN CORN BREAD
Makes two 450 g/1 lb loaves

	UK	US
225 g yellow cornmeal or polenta	8 oz	2 cups
175 g plain white flour	6 oz	$1\frac{1}{2}$ cups
15 ml baking powder	1 tbsp	
1.5 ml salt	$\frac{1}{4}$ tsp	
3 eggs		
45 ml corn oil	3 tbsp	
150 ml milk	$\frac{1}{4}$ pt	$\frac{1}{2}$ cup + 2 tbsp
One 326 g can whole sweetcorn kernels, drained	$11\frac{1}{2}$ oz can	

Sift together into a bowl the cornmeal, flour and baking powder. Add the salt. In a second bowl, beat the eggs, oil and milk. Stir the liquids into the dry ingredients. Pound the sweetcorn kernels to break them up, and add them to the mixture. Grease two loaf tins (pans) about 180 × 80 × 55 mm/7 × $3\frac{1}{2}$ × $2\frac{1}{4}$ in in size.

Turn half the mixture into each. Level the tops and cover tightly with foil. Put the tins (pans) into an oval pot-roaster or deep roasting tin (pan), and fill with enough hot water to come half-way up the sides of the tins (pans). Put on the lid of a pot-roaster, or cover a roasting tin (pan) tightly with foil. Place over moderate heat, and bring the water to simmering point. Reduce the heat and simmer for 2 hours, topping up with extra boiling water if needed.

Cool in the tins (pans). Turn onto a wire rack, and leave to stand, uncovered, for several hours or overnight. Store in an airtight container for 24 hours before cutting. Eat within 48 hours after making the bread. Do not freeze.

OATCAKES
Makes 8

	UK	US
175 g fine oatmeal	6 oz	1½ cups
50 g plain white flour	2 oz	½ cup
2.5 ml salt	½ tsp	
1.5 ml bicarbonate of soda (baking soda)	¼ tsp	
25 g margarine or bacon fat	1 oz	2 tbsp
50–125 ml hot water	2–4 fl oz	¼–½ cup as needed

Fine oatmeal for dusting

Mix together the oatmeal, flour, salt and soda. Melt the fat and work it in with enough hot water to make a stiff dough. Turn onto a board dusted with oatmeal, and knead well. Divide into 2 equal portions, and roll each out into a neat circle, as thinly as possible. Cut each into 4 quarters.

Place on an ungreased baking sheet dusted with oatmeal. Bake at 180°C/350°F/Gas 4 for 20 minutes or until the edges curl. Cool on the sheets, and store in an airtight tin.

Serve lightly toasted or cold.

SEMI-SWEET FRUIT BREAD
Makes two 450 g/1 lb loaves

	UK	US
225 ml milk or semi-skimmed milk	8 fl oz	1 cup
30 ml margarine	2 tbsp	
45 ml dark soft brown sugar	3 tbsp	
15 ml plain dried yeast	1 tbsp	
50 ml lukewarm water	2 fl oz	¼ cup
400 g 85% extraction flour or half wholemeal (whole wheat) and half white flour	14 oz	3½ cups
5 ml salt (optional)	1 tsp	
50 g Brazil or other nut flakes	2 oz	½ cup
125 g seedless raisins or	4 oz	⅔ cup
50 g chopped or mixed peel	2 oz	½ cup

Grease two 180 × 90 mm/7 × 3½ in loaf pans. Put the milk, fat and sugar in a saucepan, bring to simmering point, then cool to lukewarm. Sprinkle the yeast on the water in a cup, and leave until frothy. Meanwhile, sift the flours and salt together into a large bowl, returning any bran in the sifter to the mixture. Make a well in the centre. Pour the lukewarm milk mixture into the yeast liquid, and pour them into the well in the flour. Stir with a wooden spoon to make a sticky dough. Stir or work in the nuts and fruit or peel. Sprinkle with extra flour, and knead it by hand for a few minutes to make a dough which leaves the sides of the bowl cleanly. Take it out of the bowl. Film the inside of the bowl with oil, and replace the dough. Turn it over to film it with oil, cover it loosely with a cloth over the bowl, and leave it in a warm place until doubled in bulk. On a lightly floured surface, divide it into two equal portions, and shape them into oblongs. Place them in the pans. Level the tops. Leave in a warm place until the dough reaches the tops of the pans. Bake at 200°C/400°F/Gas 6 for about 35 minutes or until the loaves sound hollow when tapped on the bottom. Cool on a wire rack, or balanced across the tops of the pans.

NOTES

1) If you have no pans of this size, place the two oblongs of dough on a greased baking sheet well spaced apart. Leave them to rise for 35 minutes, then bake on the sheet.

2) If you wish, you can give the risen loaves a spicy crust just before baking, by brushing them lightly with margarine, then sprinkling them with a mixture of sugar and ground mixed spice in the proportion of 5 ml/ 1 tsp sugar to 1.5 ml/$\frac{1}{4}$ tsp spice.

APPLESAUCE CAKE
Makes one 225 mm/9 in layer cake

	UK	US
225 g soft brown sugar	8 oz	1 cup
125 g margarine	4 oz	$\frac{1}{2}$ cup
1 egg		
200 g 81% or 85% extraction flour or wholemeal (whole wheat) and white flour, mixed	7 oz	1$\frac{3}{4}$ cups
175 g raisins	6 oz	1 cup
125 g flaked almonds (optional)	4 oz	1 cup
2.5 ml salt	$\frac{1}{2}$ tsp	
5 ml bicarbonate of soda (baking soda)	1 tsp	
5 ml ground cinnamon	1 tsp	
2.5 ml ground cloves	$\frac{1}{2}$ tsp	

225 g lightly sweetened apple		
sauce	8 oz	1 cup
Extra apple sauce for filling		

Sift the sugar, cream the fat, and beat them together until light and fluffy. Beat in the egg. Turn the flour into a bowl with the salt, soda, and both spices. Stir these dry goods into the batter mixture, and add the fruit and nuts.

Warm the apple sauce and beat it in. Turn the mixture into two greased layer tins (pans). Bake for 25–35 minutes at 190°C/375°F/Gas 5. Cool on a wire rack, then sandwich with well-drained apple sauce.

CARROT CAKE

Makes one 200–210 mm/8–8½ in round or square cake

	UK	US
125 ml warmed honey	4 fl oz	½ cup
50 g melted margarine	2 oz	¼ cup
2 eggs		
150 ml natural yoghurt	¼ pt	½ cup + 2 tbsp
250 g young carrots, finely grated		
(4–5 carrots)	9 oz	
50 g flaked almonds (optional)	2 oz	½ cup
75 g wholemeal (whole wheat)		
flour	3 oz	⅓ cup
75 g white flour	3 oz	⅓ cup
2.5 ml salt	½ tsp	
2.5 ml bicarbonate of soda (baking		
soda)	½ tsp	
10 ml ground cinnamon or nutmeg	2 tsp	

Warm your honey-pot and margarine in the oven set to heat to 150°C/ 300°F/Gas 2. Beat the eggs in a mixing bowl, then beat in the yoghurt, honey and melted fat. Stir in the grated carrots and the nuts if you use them. Sift all the remaining ingredients together, and return any bran in the sifter to the dry mixture. Stir it into the carrot mixture without beating. Turn the mixture into a well-greased round or square tin, 200–210 mm/8–8½ in diameter. Bake at the temperature above for 1¼–1½ hours. Cool for 30 minutes in the tin, then finish cooling on a wire rack. Keeps well in an airtight tin.

RAISIN DROP CAKES
Makes 30

	UK	US
125 g margarine	4 oz	½ cup
75 g brown sugar	3 oz	
1 egg		
125 g 85% extraction flour	4 oz	1 cup
Pinch of salt		
2.5 ml bicarbonate of soda (baking soda)	½ tsp	
2.5 ml ground cinnamon	½ tsp	
2.5 ml ground cloves	½ tsp	
50 g Quaker Oats	2 oz	½ cup (heaped)
75 g raisins	3 oz	½ cup
65 ml water	⅛ pt	5 tbsp
50 g chopped mixed nuts (optional)	2 oz	½ cup

Bring the raisins and water to the boil in a saucepan. Stir round and leave to cool while you make the cookies. Cream the fat and sugar, and beat in the egg. Dissolve the soda in 30 ml/2 tbsp of the raisin water, and beat in. Sift together and stir in the flour, salt and spices. Then stir in the oats, and nuts if you use them. Drain and add the raisins. Drop the mixture in teaspoonfuls, well spaced apart, on ungreased baking sheets (trays). Bake at 220°C/425°F/Gas 7 for 8–10 minutes. Cool on the sheets, then loosen, take off and store.

NOTE These are very easy to make and melt in the mouth if you use soft margarine and leave out the nuts. For stiffer cookies, use softened block margarine, rolled oats and nuts.

PEANUT BUTTER COOKIES
Makes 20–24

	UK	US
50 g margarine	2 oz	¼ cup
50 g crunchy peanut butter	2 oz	¼ cup
75 g dark brown sugar	3 oz	
5 ml lemon juice	1 tsp	
1 egg yolk		
75 g 85% extraction flour	3 oz	¾ cup
Pinch of ground cinnamon		

167

Pinch of ground mace
1.5 ml bicarbonate of soda (baking
   soda) $\frac{1}{4}$ tsp
1.5 ml baking powder $\frac{1}{4}$ tsp
Pinch of salt
Flour for dusting

Beat the fats and sugar together until smooth and creamy. Beat in the lemon juice and egg yolk. Sift together and stir in the flour, spices, soda, baking powder and salt. Chill until firm enough to handle. With your palm, roll small pieces into balls about 2.5 cm diameter on a lightly floured sheet of paper. Place well apart on greased and floured baking sheets, and dent the top of each ball with your thumb. Bake at 180°C/350°F/Gas 4 for 15 minutes. Loosen with a spatula, then leave to firm and cool on the sheets. Store in an airtight tin (or cookie jar).

HONEY-CINNAMON SQUARES OR BARS

Makes one 180 mm/7 in square flat slab

	UK	US
125 g low fat spread	4 oz	$\frac{1}{2}$ cup
60 ml warmed honey	4 tbsp	4 tbsp
1.5 ml ground cinnamon	$\frac{1}{4}$ tsp	$\frac{1}{4}$ tsp
125 g 100% wholemeal (whole wheat) and white flour, mixed	4 oz	1 cup
Pinch of salt		
1.5 ml bicarbonate of soda (baking soda)	$\frac{1}{4}$ tsp	

Beat the fat until soft and creamy, then beat in the honey slowly. Sift together all the remaining ingredients and beat them in, a little at a time. Chill or leave to firm up in a cool place if still semi-liquid. Turn the mixture into a greased and floured 180 mm/7 in square shallow baking tin (pan) and level the top. Bake at 180°C/350°F/Gas 4 for 15–18 minutes. Cool in the tin, then cut into squares or fingers.

DESSERTS AND SWEETS

BROWN BETTY
Serves 4–6

	UK	US
125 g soft wholemeal (whole wheat) breadcrumbs	4 oz	1½ cups
45 ml melted margarine	3 tbsp	
450 g peeled sliced apples	1 lb	2¾ cups
125 g soft brown sugar	4 oz	½ cup
1.5 ml ground cinnamon	¼ tsp	
1.5 ml grated nutmeg	¼ tsp	
1.5 ml salt	¼ tsp	
5 ml grated lemon rind	1 tsp	
30 ml lemon juice (optional)	2 tbsp	
75 g raisins (optional)	3 oz	½ cup

Mix together the breadcrumbs and melted fat. Sprinkle about half the mixture over the bottom and sides of a shallow 1.4 L/2½ pt (3 pt) deep baking dish. Cover with half the apples in an even layer. Mix together the sugar, spices, salt and rind. Sprinkle half the mixture over the apples, then sprinkle with half the lemon juice and raisins if used. Repeat the apple layer, then the layer of sugar mixture. Cover with the crumbs not yet used. Cover the dish and bake at 180°C/350°F/Gas 4 for 30 minutes. Uncover, raise the heat to 200°C/400°F/Gas 6 for 10–15 minutes until the topping is crisp and the apples are tender when pierced with a skewer. Serve hot.

OATMEAL APPLE CRUMBLE
Serves 4–6

	UK	US
600 g cooking apples	1¼ lb	
60 ml water	4 tbsp	
Grated rind of ½ lemon		
50 g raisins	2 oz	⅓ cup
Sugar to taste		
25 g margarine	1 oz	⅛ cup
150 g medium oatmeal	5 oz	
50 g sugar	2 oz	¼ cup
1.5 ml ground ginger	¼ tsp	

Peel, core and chop the apples. Put in a saucepan with the water, lemon rind and raisins and with a little sugar (if the apples are tart). Cover, and simmer until soft. Turn into a shallow, bake-and-serve dish or flan case, 180–190 mm/7–7½ in diameter in an even layer. Melt the fat and mix it with the oatmeal, sugar and ginger to make a crumbly mixture. Sprinkle it over the apples and press down lightly. Bake at 180°C/350°F/Gas 4 for 30 minutes or until the topping is light gold.

BAKED APPLES FILLED WITH RAISINS
Single helping(s)

	UK	US as UK
1 large cooking apple		
15–30 ml raisins	1–2 tbsp	
Pinch of ground cinnamon		
15 ml black treacle (molasses)	1 tbsp	
30 ml orange juice	2 tbsp	

Core the apple without peeling it. Slit the skin horizontally around the middle. Place it in a small ovenproof shallow bowl or deep saucer. Mix together the raisins and cinnamon. Fill into the core-hole of the apple. Pour the treacle molasses on top of the apple and the orange juice in the saucer around it.

Bake at 190°C/375°F/Gas 5 for about 40 minutes. Pour a little extra orange juice over the apple before serving.

NOTE If you wish, you can stuff the apple with a mixture of raisins and chopped almonds, and use a blackcurrant fruit drink to pour over the apple after baking. Omit the cinnamon.

TOFU FRUIT FOOL
Single helpings(s)

This is a delicious way to use ripe sweet fruit but it is not possible to give definite quantities because fruits vary so much in flavour. Sharp or strongly flavoured fruit may need twice as much tofu as bland fruits require.

Make a fruit purée, using about 50 g/2 oz strongly flavoured fruit, such as apricots or blackcurrants, or 125 g/4 oz blander fruit, such as peaches, per person. Ripe soft and stone fruits do not need cooking. Hull if needed, and remove stones or large seeds. Take off tough skins, e.g. melon. Then sieve the fruit into a bowl, using a nylon sieve. Harder fruits such as apples will need blanching until just soft and may need sweetening before sieving. Flavour bland fruits, e.g. peaches or melon, with 5 ml/1 tsp orange or lemon juice (per 25 g/4 oz fruit) when sieving.

Since some fruits discolour rapidly when sieved, immediately beat into the purée some drained long-life, silken tofu. Start by adding a quarter of the weight of the whole fruit, that is 25 g/1 oz tofu to 125 g/4 oz fruit, in the case of bland fruit; sharp-flavoured fruit may need the same weight of tofu as of fruit or even more. This is because silken tofu has a more junket-like consistency than cream or custard and no flavour of its own. Having added the initial quantity of tofu, taste the mixture and add more tofu if required. When the mixture is quite smooth, chill if possible. Serve in individual glasses with a tiny sprig of mint or a few shreds of orange peel on top.

WINTER FRUIT SALAD
Serves 6

	UK	US
125 g prunes	4 oz	
125 g dried apricots	4 oz	
125 g dried figs	4 oz	
50 g dried apple rings	2 oz	
350 ml water	12 fl oz	$1\frac{1}{2}$ cups
50 g raisins	2 oz	$\frac{1}{3}$ cup
40 g almond or Brazil nut flakes	$1\frac{1}{2}$ oz	$\frac{2}{3}$ cup
25 g walnut pieces, cut into bits	1 oz	$\frac{1}{4}$ cup
30 ml dark brown sugar	2 tbsp	
30 ml extra water	2 tbsp	

Put the prunes, apricots, figs and apple rings in a bowl, cover with the water and soak for 48 hours, turning the fruit over occasionally. Cut the softened fruit into small pieces, removing the prune stones. Do not discard the liquid. Return the fruit to the bowl, and add the nuts and raisins. Dissolve the sugar in the extra water over low heat, and pour it over the salad. Cool and chill before serving.

SUMMER PUDDING
Serves 6

	UK	US as UK
8–9 slices dryish whole-grain bread (from a large tin loaf) with crusts removed		
700 g mixed soft fruits, e.g. raspberries, currants (black or red) ripe cherries	1½ lb	
60 ml honey	4 tbsp	

Line the bottom of an 850 ml/1½ pt (3¾ cup) pudding basin with 1 or 2 slices of bread. Then line the sides of the basin, fitting the bread slices closely together, without gaps between them. Prepare and wash the fruit, and put into a pan with the honey. Cook for 2–3 minutes until the juices run.

Spoon the fruit and juice into the bread-lined basin, and cover with more bread. Put a plate on the pudding and a heavy tin or jar on top to weight it down. Leave it in a refrigerator or cool place for 8–12 hours. Turn the pudding out onto a serving plate.

This can make an easy, lovely pudding FOR ONE PERSON. Use a 275 ml/½ pt (1¼ cup) basin, and line it with 4 slices of leftover bread from a large tin loaf. Use about 275 ml/½ pt (1¼ cups) stewed or canned soft fruit, and 15–20 ml/3–4 tsp honey or to taste.

HOME-MADE CUSTARD ICE-CREAM (Economical)
Serves 4

	UK	US
30 ml custard powder	2 tbsp	
575 ml milk	1 pt	2½ cups
75 g sugar	3 oz	⅓ cup

150 ml double (heavy) cream (see note)	$\frac{1}{4}$ pt	$\frac{1}{2}$ cup + 2 tbsp
5 ml vanilla essence	1 tsp	

Blend the custard powder to a cream with a little of the milk. Heat the rest of the milk to simmering point, and slowly stir it into the custard mixture. Return to the pan, and simmer, stirring constantly, until very thick. Cool, covered with damp paper. Stir from time to time while cooling, to prevent a skin forming.

When quite cold, make the ice cream. If you have no freezer, use ice-making trays without separators, and clear the ice-making compartment. Turn a home freezer to the fast-freeze setting.

Put the cream in a separate bowl, and whisk it until semi-stiff. Fold it into the custard with the essence. Turn into a suitable container. Chill, then freeze until thick at the edges and mushy in the middle. Turn into a bowl, and beat hard until the same consistency all through. Return to the freezing container(s) and freeze until firm.

NOTE For extra economy, use a mixture of equal quantities of sieved cottage cheese and a fruit yoghurt, sieved to pulp any solid bits, instead of cream. Omit the essence.

FRESH ORANGE CHEESECAKE (low fat)
Serves 4–6

	UK	US
Base		
175 g digestive biscuit crumbs	6 oz	
40 g low-fat spread	$1\frac{1}{2}$ oz	3 tbsp
15 ml honey	1 tbsp	
Filling		
1 orange		
15 g gelatine	1 oz or 1 envelope	
30 ml warmed honey	2 tbsp	
225 g low fat soft cheese	8 oz	1 cup
150 ml natural yoghurt	$\frac{1}{4}$ pt	$\frac{1}{2}$ cup + 2 tbsp
1 orange for decoration (see method)		

Grease the inside of a 150 mm/6 in cake tin (pan) with a loose bottom. Make sure the crumbs are fine and even. Melt the fat and honey together, and beat into the crumbs in a bowl. Press the mixture over the base and 50 mm/2 in of the sides of the tin (pan); bake at 180°C/350°F/Gas 4 for 10 minutes. Cool completely.

Grate the rind of the orange fairly coarsely. Squeeze but do not strain the juice. Soften the gelatine in the orange juice, then stand the container in very hot water and stir until the gelatine dissolves. Warm the honey. Beat together the cheese and yoghurt until quite smooth, then beat in the grated rind, honey and gelatine mixture. Pour into the prepared case, and chill overnight.

Cover the cheesecake lightly with a round of greaseproof paper and trim the top edges of the crumb case. If you wish, crumble and keep any baked crumbs you take off to sprinkle over the orange topping (or use instead of the orange topping if you have enough, and save the second orange).

Shortly before serving, remove the cheesecake from the tin. Peel the orange for decoration, divide it into segments and skin them. Arrange them in a decorative pattern on the cheesecake.

CITRUS CHEESECAKE
Serves 8–10

	UK	US
Base		
150 g fine plain biscuit (cracker) crumbs	6 oz	
30 ml dried skimmed milk powder	2 tbsp	
50 g low-fat spread or polyunsaturated margarine	2 oz	$\frac{1}{4}$ cup
Filling		
45 ml orange juice	3 tbsp	
15 g powdered gelatine	$\frac{1}{2}$ oz	1 envelope
30 ml lemon juice	2 tbsp	
250 g low-fat smooth soft cheese	12 oz	$1\frac{1}{2}$ cups
50 g white sugar	2 oz	$\frac{1}{3}$–$\frac{1}{2}$ cup
2 eggs, separated		
Dried skimmed milk powder to make 1.1 L liquid if made up	to make 2 pt	to make 5 cups
Topping		
Grated orange rind or Melba toast crumbs and a little sugar		

Lightly grease the inside of a square 200 mm/8 in cake tin (pan) with a loose base. Crush the biscuits (crackers) to fine even crumbs. Mix in the dried skimmed milk powder, then beat in the fat until the crumbs stick together. Press in an even layer all over the base of the tin (pan). Chill while making the filling.

Put the orange juice in a heatproof jug, and stir in the gelatine slowly, to avoid clotting. Stand the jug in a pan of hot water and stir until the gelatine dissolves. Off the heat, add the lemon juice. Keep aside. Beat together the cheese, sugar and egg yolks until they hold soft peaks. Make up the dried skimmed milk powder with 275 ml/$\frac{1}{2}$ pt/1$\frac{1}{4}$ cups cold water, taking care not to make lumps.

Add to the cheese mixture first half the gelatine, then half the milk liquid, followed by the remaining gelatine and milk mixture. Fold in the whisked egg whites. Pour onto the chilled crumb base, and leave for 4–6 hours to set.

Decorate with rind or crumbs as you wish.

APRICOT PASTE BALLS
Makes 24 balls

	UK	US
250 g dried apricots	9 oz	1$\frac{1}{2}$ cups
175 g desiccated (unsweetened) coconut	6 oz	1$\frac{1}{2}$ cups
5 ml finely grated (minced) orange rind	1 tsp	1 tsp
5 ml finely grated (minced) lemon rind	1 tsp	1 tsp
30 ml orange juice	2 tbsp	2 tbsp
25 g desiccated (unsweetened) coconut for rolling	1 oz	$\frac{1}{4}$ cup

Wash the apricots, cover with boiling water, and leave to stand for 5 minutes. Drain them, and mix with the coconut in a mortar or food mill (see note).

Pound or grind until the apricots are pasty. Add the orange and lemon rind and the orange juice. Process again to blend in. Chill or leave in a cold place until firm if required.

Shape into 24 small balls, and leave at room temperature for 2 hours, then roll them in coconut. Keep in a covered container in a refrigerator.

NOTE If you have not got a pestle and mortar or food processor, you could mince (grind) the fruit and coconut together, twice if necessary.

MOCHA TRUFFLES
Makes 12

	UK	US as UK
22 ml cocoa powder	1½ tbsp	
15 ml instant coffee powder	1 tbsp	
30 ml honey or golden syrup (light molasses)	2 tbsp	
30 ml low-fat spread	2 tbsp	
40 g dried skimmed milk powder, 'sifted	1½ oz	
Desiccated unsweetened coconut		

Mix together the cocoa powder and instant coffee in a small saucepan. Add the syrup. Stir over low heat until blended and smooth. Off the heat, stir in the fat and dried milk powder until you have a smooth paste. Chill in a refrigerator or cold place overnight. Roll the mixture between your hands into 12 small balls. On a sheet of paper, roll the balls in desiccated coconut, coating thoroughly. Keep chilled.

APPENDIX I:
GOOD FOODS TO CHOOSE

Choose from these lists foods which are cheap at the time you want to buy them.

PROTEINS

Good sources
Liver and kidneys.
Stewing lamb (cut off excess fat).
Stewing beef (cut off excess fat).
Mince (ground beef).
Chicken.
Turkey.
Oily fish.
White fish.
Milk, yoghurt.
Cheese (hard, soft or cottage).
Eggs (up to 3 a week per person).
Soya beans.
Lentils.
Nuts, especially peanuts, almonds, Brazil nuts.

Fair sources
Use these with one of the foods on the left:
Potatoes (especially with eggs – leave skins on).
Porridge oats, oatmeal (used dry).
Wholemeal (whole wheat) breakfast cereals.
Brown rice.
Green peas, dried peas.
Flageolet (lima) beans and broad (fava) beans/all dried beans.
Sesame seeds.

CARBOHYDRATE

All starchy foods, especially:
Whole-grain foods, including rice and pasta.
Wholemeal (whole wheat) bread, flours, and oatmeal, cornmeal etc.

Vegetables such as potatoes, parsnips, peas, broad beans and dried beans.
Fruits, especially sweet raw fruits such as apples, cherries.
Dried fruits.
NOTE Avoid sugary foods.

FATS
Margarine (polyunsaturated if possible) especially with added vitamins.
Corn oil.
Sunflower oil.
Safflower oil.
Soya oil.
Ground nut oil.
Oily fish.
Nuts.
Cheese (not cream cheese or cheese spreads).
Eggs (see above).
NOTE Remember the 'hidden' saturated fat in meats, eggs.

SPECIAL VITAMIN AND MINERAL VALUE
Every day:
*Wholegrain cereals.
*Dark green vegetables, e.g. cabbage, spinach.
*Potatoes, tomatoes, one citrus fruit (and one soft fruit when in season).

Once a week:
Liver.
Oily fish.
Peas.
Beans (flageolet (lima), broad (fava), and dried beans).
Carrots.
Milk and/or a milk product, e.g. yoghurt, hard, soft or cottage cheese.

Other meats, fish, egg, yeast, lentils, nuts, raw and milk products also contain valuable quantities of various vitamins and minerals, varying with the season, the product's age and how it has been processed; the foods above are not the only ones. However, you should use the ones above as your basic 'backstop' types of food. Make sure you include them all in your diet at least once a week, and have the ones marked with an asterisk EVERY DAY. (See also the list on page 55). Then you can use other foods to get the rest of your vitamins and minerals freely.

When using commercially fortified foods and drinks, look at the labels to make sure you want the whole 'package'. You may not want grapefruit juice fortified with vitamin C if it is also heavily sweetened, for instance.

APPENDIX II:
USEFUL TABLES

TABLE 1: RECOMMENDED DAILY AMOUNTS OF FOOD ENERGY AND PROTEIN FOR POPULATION GROUPS IN THE UNITED KINGDOM

Age range in years	Energy Usage	Calories (Kcal)	Protein (in grams)
Boys			
1		1200	30
2		1400	35
3–4		1560	39
5–6		1740	43
7–8		1980	49
9–11		2280	57
12–14		2640	66
15–17		2880	72
Girls			
1		1100	27
2		1300	32
3–4		1500	37
5–6		1680	42
7–8		1900	47
9–11		2050	51
12–14		2150	53
15–17		2150	53
Men			
18–34	sedentary	2510	63
	moderately active	2900	72
	very active	3350	84
35–64	sedentary	2400	60
	moderately active	2750	69
	very active	3350	84
65–74 }	assuming a sedentary life	2400	60
75 + }		2150	54
Women			
18–54	most occupations	2150	54
	very active	2500	62
55–74 }	assuming a sedentary life	1900	47
75 + }		1680	42
	pregnancy	2400	60
	lactation	2750	69

Figures from *Recommended Daily Amounts of Food Energy and Nutrients for Groups of People in the United Kingdom* (Report by the Committee on Medical Aspects of Food Policy. Report on Health and Social Subjects 15. Dept of Health and Social Security.) Crown Copyright. 1979. (Reproduced by permission of H.M.S.O.)

180

**TABLE 2: SOME COMMON RAW FOODS: 100-GRAM PORTIONS –
AVERAGE CARBOHYDRATE / DIETARY FIBRE CONTENT (GRAMS)**

Food	Sugar	Starch	Total Carbohydrate	Dietary Fibre
Ice cream – dairy	22.6	2.2	24.8	–
Sugar	105.0	0	105.0	0.0
Syrup	79.0	0	79.0	0.0
Jam fruit + edible seeds	69.0	0	69.0	1.1
Potatoes – old, raw	0.5	20.3	20.8	2.1
Baked beans	5.2	5.1	10.3	7.3
White bread	1.8	47.9	49.7	2.7
Wholemeal bread	2.1	39.7	41.8	8.5
Oatmeal	0	72.8	72.8	7.0
Chocolate biscuits (full-coated)	43.4	24.0	67.4	3.1
Orange – raw	8.5	0	8.5	2.0
Orange squash, without water	28.5	0	28.5	0.0
Banana	16.2	3.0	19.2	3.4
Peaches, canned in syrup	22.9	0	22.9	1.0
Tomato soup – cream of, canned, ready to serve	2.6	3.3	5.9	–

The Composition of Foods by A.A. Paul & D.A.T. Southgate (McCance and Widdowson) 4th edition. H.M.S.O. (Reproduced by permission of H.M.S.O.)

TABLE 3: APPROXIMATE FAT CONTENT OF SOME RAW FOODS (IN 100-GRAM/3½-OZ PORTIONS)

Food	Grams of fat
Vegetable cooking oils	99.9
Lard	99.0
Margarine with some animal fat	81.0
Margarine without animal fat	81.0
Butter	82.0
Pork – lean, average	7.1
Beef – lean, average	4.6
Chicken (white meat) – average	3.2
Herring – average*	18.5
Canned salmon	8.2
Whole eggs	10.9
Cheddar cheese	33.5
Milk	3.8
Wholemeal bread	2.7
White bread	1.7
Potatoes	0.1

NOTE *Range 1985 = 5 g/100 g (February–April) – 20 g/100 g (July–October)

Figures adapted from *Manual of Nutrition*. Reference Book 342. 8th edition. H.M.S.O. 1978. (Reproduced by permission of H.M.S.O.)

APPENDIX III:
NOTES ON THE RECIPE
INGREDIENTS AND TERMS USED
IN THIS BOOK

American names and measures are given in brackets after the metric and UK ones.

1) Breads and flours.

The terms *wholemeal* and *wholewheat* are used interchangeably in this book to mean 100 per cent *whole wheat* flour or its products. Both contain all the 'germ' and bran of the whole wheat grain.

When you buy bread or flour, always try to get products labelled as 100 per cent extraction, preferably stone ground. (Stone grinding is thought to preserve the nutrients in the grain better than modern roller milling.) The only exceptions are (a) when you want to bake light cakes or pastry; (b) if you are trying to introduce your family to whole-grain foods. In these cases, use a *high extraction* flour (generally 81 per cent or 85 per cent) which contain quite a lot of their nutrients although not all. For bread-making, use *strong flour* in the UK, *bread flour* in the USA. Otherwise, use *plain flour (all purpose* flour). In the UK, avoid *wheatmeal* and *brown* breads and flours unless the ingredient list on the label satisfies you that they are made from the whole grain; they need not be.

If you use *cornmeal* (sometimes called by the Italian name *polenta* in the UK) try to get unrefined, stone-ground or water-ground cornmeal from a Health Food store instead of refined supermarket cornmeal which is low in nutrients and makes crumbly breads. Add some wheat flour to it when baking, and to whole-grain flours such as rye, oat or barley flour. Their products do not rise as well as wheat flour products. Note that they do not keep quite as well either.

2) Margarine

Government and medical authorities in both the UK and USA recommend using polyunsaturated fats. The term *polyunsaturated* has not been used in the recipes for space reasons, but you should use margarine (and cooking fat) made only from polyunsaturated fats and oils if possible. Note that the term 'high in polyunsaturates' on a container label or wrapper does not mean that *only* unsaturated fats and oils have been used to make the product; some saturated fats are included.

3) Oil

No particular type of oil has been recommended in the recipes because the cheapest suitable types vary from place to place. Any pure vegetable oil high in polyunsaturated fatty acids is generally suitable for both grilling and baking. Corn, sunflower and groundnut oil, for instance, are all good. Olive oil and walnut oil are the least suitable for general use among the low-saturate oils because they are generally the most expensive, least stable, and have a distinctive flavour. Coconut oil and cottonseed oil are unsuitable. Always check the label on a container of oil to make sure it specifies that the content is a pure, not a blended oil. Flora (Promise) Oil is a typical high-grade suitable vegetable oil.

4) Low-fat spread

Usually describes a blend of vegetable oils, buttermilk, gelatine and salt flavoured and coloured to taste and look like butter or margarine, but with only about half the fat and calories. There are various brands of which one, Outline, is sold in the United States as Diet Imperial.

5) Low-fat soft cheese

A soft cheese made with dairy ingredients and designed to taste like light mild soft cream-style cheeses such as Philadelphia soft cheese, but with less than half the normal fat and calories. The low-fat cheese is softer and less sharply flavoured than British curd cheese or Quark cheese. If you cannot get it, use sieved cottage cheese with a little dried skimmed milk powder beaten into it.

Similar low-fat cottage cheeses and yoghurts, variously flavoured, are also available.

6) Low-fat hard cheese

In a mature, hard English or American cheese, such as mature Cheddar or American sharp cheese, the fat and calories are tight-packed with very little moisture. Cheeses which are comparatively young contain more moisture so have less fat and fewer calories in the same space. Some hard cheeses similar to Cheddar and Cheshire are made in Britain which have only half the fat content of the traditional cheeses. There are several brands; they tend to be more crumbly than the traditional hard cheeses, but are good for making sauces or toppings, in salads etc.

7) Yoghurt

When the word *yoghurt* is used by itself in a recipe, it means low-fat yoghurt made largely with skimmed milk. *Natural yoghurt* means that no other product flavour has been added to the yoghurt. Full-fat Greek or Turkish yoghurt has not been used in the recipes.

8) Sugar

All white sugars are heavily refined, but some brands of soft brown and golden crystalline sugar are claimed to be less so. They are sold in the UK as raw or natural, unrefined sugar or as Barbados or Muscovado sugars. They are usually more expensive than white sugars but have a markedly better, more vital flavour than other sugars. For uncooked dishes, you can use one of the low-sugar or sugarless sweeteners on the market but remember that most are chemical additives.

9) Honey

Clear honey is the most convenient to use in cooking, but like any honey is very costly compared with some cheaper sweeteners such as wholefruit jams (see page 26). It has been used in some of the baking recipes in this book for its spreading and mixing quality, and for the distinctive sweetness that even a small quantity offers.

10) Gelatine

Powdered, i.e. granulated, unflavoured gelatine has been used in the recipes. If you are a strict vegetarian, you can use agar-agar instead, but it is more expensive.

11) Salt

Table salt has magnesium carbonate added, to make it run freely. Although you should, in general, try to cut down your use of salt, it may be convenient to keep in stock, so that you can use a pinch in your baked goods instead of grinding rock crystal or sea salt. These salts, although better flavoured, are more expensive to use.

USEFUL READING

The cookery books in the following lists all contain useful recipes. Adapt the products to recommended ones if necessary; for instance, you can nearly always use polyunsaturated margarine instead of butter. Forget the fried dishes and any very sugary recipes. Watch the eggs in any pre-1980 books you use.

GREAT BRITAIN
Cookery Books

Ardley, Bridget, *The Austerity Cookbook*, Latimer 1975 (realistic economy ideas).

Dixon, Pamela, *Pulse Cookery*, Thorsons 1980 (interesting recipes for peas/beans/lentils).

Dixon, Susan, and Black, Maggie (eds), *Mrs Beeton's Cookery and Household Management*, Ward Lock 1980 (standard basic recipes).

Elliot, Rose, *Not Just A Load Of Old Lentils*, Fontana 1976, and *Simply Delicious*, Fontana 1977 (wise commonsense advice/outstanding vegetarian recipes).

Fitzgibbon, Theodora, *Making The Most Of It*, Hutchinson 1978 (excellent economy ideas/recipes).

Hanssen, Maurice, *Country Kitchen Recipes With Wholemeal Flour*, Thorsons 1979 (practical range of baked goods and main dishes).

Reekie, Jennie, *Everything Raw*, Penguin 1978.

Rogers, Jenny (ed), *The Taste of Health – The BBC Guide to Healthy Cooking*, BBC 1985.

BRITISH GOVERNMENT AND OTHER INFORMATIONAL PUBLICATIONS

Manual of Nutrition, Reference Book 342, 8th edition prepared by David Buss and Jean Robertson 1976. Reprinted 1984. Ministry of Agriculture, Fisheries and Food, HMSO.

Look At The Label, Central Office of Information for the Ministry of
Agriculture, Fisheries and Food 1984. (Ministry of Agriculture,
Fisheries and Food Publications Unit, Lion House, Willowburn
Trading Estate, Alnwick, Northumberland NE66 2PE, UK.)
Proposals For Nutritional Guidelines for Health Education in Britain,
Working Party of the National Advisory Committee on Nutrition
Education for the Health Education Council of the Department of
Health and Social Security 1983.
Davis, Adelle, *Let's Eat Right To Keep Fit*, Unwin Paperbacks 1979.
Davis, Adelle, *Let's Have Healthy Children*, Unwin Paperbacks 1981.
Tudge, Colin, *The Food Connection – The BBC Guide to Healthy
Eating*, BBC 1985.

USA COOKERY BOOKS

Albright, Nancy, *The Rodale Cookbook*, Rodale Press Book Division
1973 (general health foods cookbook), and *Rodale's Naturally Great
Foods Cookbook*, Rodale Books 1977.
Hewitt, Jean, *The New York Times Natural Foods Cookbook*,
Quadrangle 1971.
Kinderlehrer, Jane, *Confessions of a Sneaky Organic Cook*, Rodale
Press Inc. 1975 (information and recipes on healthy eating).
Levinson, Leonard, *The Live Longer Cookbook*, Bantam Books 1973
(recipes for healthy eating).
McKinnell, Joyce, *Vegetarian Gourmet Cookbook*, Wilshire Book Co.
1972.
Robertson, Laurel, Flinders, Carol, and Godfrey, Bronwen, *Laurel's
Kitchen*, Nilgiri Press 1976 (authoritative information on the
vegetarian diet as well as recipes).
Shurtleff, W., and Aoyagi, A., *The Book of Tofu*, Ballantyne, NY 1979
(information and recipes).
Wade, Carlson, *the Book of Bran*, Pyramid Publications 1976 (useful
information as well as recipes).

US GOVERNMENT AND OTHER INFORMATIONAL
PUBLICATIONS
Dietary Goals for the United States, Senate Select Committee on
Nutrition and Human Needs, US Senate, February 1977.
GPO No. 052-070-03913-2. Washington DC.
Adams, Catherine, F., *Nutritive Value of American Foods in Common*

Units, Agriculture Handbook No. 456, US Dept of Agriculture, Washington, Govt. Printing office 1975.

Goodhart, Robert S., and Shils, Maurice E. (eds), *Modern Nutrition in Health and Disease,* Dietotherapy, Lea and Debiger 1973.

Jacobson, Michael, *Eater's Digest – The Consumer's Fact-Book of Food Additives,* Doubleday, Anchor Books 1972.

Jacobson, Michael, *Nutrition Scoreboard,* Avon, New York 1975.

Jacobson, Michael, and Lerza, Catherine, *Food for People, Not for Profit,* Ballantyne, NY 1975.

Lappe, F.M., *Diet for a Small Planet,* Ballantyne, NY 1975.

The Barbara Kraus Guide to Fiber in Food, Signet Books, New American Library 1975 (tables).

AUSTRALIA

Cookery Books
Phillips, Dr David A., *New Dimensions Recipe Book*
Prendergast, Marie, *Cooking for Your Life*

Informational Publications
Phillips, Dr David A., *Guide to Nutritional Factors in Food.*
Porter, Suzanne, *It's Only Natural.*
Stafford, Julie, *Taste of Life.*

INDEX

References in *italics* are to recipes.